The Great Guitarists 1

Printed and bound in Great Britain by Antony Rowe Limited, Chippenham, Wiltshire

Published in the UK by SMT, an imprint of Sanctuary Publishing Limited, Sanctuary House, 45–53 Sinclair Road, London W14 0NS, United Kingdom

www.sanctuarypublishing.com

ISBN: 1-86074-244-0

In addition to the artist's in this book, Ivor considered as important innovators in the world of jazz guitar: Oscar Aleman, Barry Galbraith, Tadd Dameron, Laurindo Almeida, Mary Osborne, Ike Isaacs, Esmond Selwyn, Frank Evans, Charlie Byrd, Mundell Lowe, Attila Zoller, Hank Garland, Jimmy Wyble, Pat Martino, Pat Metheny, Larry Carlton, Larry Coryell and Emily Remler are not listed within these pages. All of these artists and their music can be found in the first edition of this book, published in 1994 by Music Maker Books Ltd, Alexander House, Forehill, Cambridgeshire CB7 4AF, UK. Retail price £250

The Great Jazz Guitarists 1

Ivor Mairants

smt

Also by Ivor Mairants and available from SMT:

The Great Jazz Guitarists 2

ACKNOWLEDGEMENTS

First, I wish to acknowledge the work of Cyril Howard and my daughter Valerie for reading and correcting my rough texts. My thanks go next to Maurice Summerfield for sending me some tapes I needed and for his general goodwill. Thanks also to Adrian Ingram for introducing me to two of his pupils: Graham Mercer, who offered a special interest in the solos of Eric Clapton, and Alan Mason, who provided a working basis of Allan Holdsworth's 'Three Sheets To The Wind'. Thanks also go to the following musicians who relieved me of some of the work with their transcriptions: Len Hunter for the solos by Dave Goldberg, Chet Atkins, John McLaughlin, Les Paul's 'How High The Moon' and George Benson; Barnaby Leons-Marder for 'They Can't Take That Away From Me' and 'Catch Me'; and James Nye for solos by Louis Stewart and Ted Greene. The above solos were personally rearranged, edited and fingered for guitar. Thanks finally to Penny Braybrooke and Cliff Douse for their work in producing and editing this book.

Ivor Mairants, 1994

This work is the result of four years' concentrated research and the culmintation of many years of dedicated, inspired and inspiring work on guitar music.

In addition to a performing career of some 60 years, always at the top of his profession, Ivor was committed to teaching. He had a positively missionary zeal in spreading knowledge of and enthusiasm for the guitar and was generous in his admiration for both his predecessors and his successors.

We are very pleased to see this great encyclopaedia of jazz guitar being made available to a new generation of enthusiasts.

Lily and Valerie Mairants, 2002

ABOUT THE AUTHOR

Born on 18 July 1908, Ivor Mairants took up music at the age of 17, playing the banjo. He had no formal musical training, and only began playing the guitar when he became a professional musician and joined Percival Mackay's band, opening on the stage of the old Alhambra Music Hall in Leicester Square, London.

He went on to appear as featured guitarist with famous dance bands of the '30s, including Roy Fox, Ambrose, Lew Stone and Bert Firman, and worked with Gaumont British Films, under Louis Levy. He also recorded with Ben Frankel, Benny Carter, Muir Matheson, Josh White, Beniamino Gigli, Phil Green, Stanley Black, Geoff Love and Julie London.

Between 1940 and 1952, with Geraldo and his orchestra, he became the most featured guitarist on the BBC, and in around the same period he topped the guitar poll in *Melody Maker* (a former British weekly music magazine) and led The Ivor Mairants Guitar Group.

He is the author of many guitar works, and also recorded his own compositions as duets with Albert Harris for Brunswick and later released solo-guitar compositions with The Geraldo Orchestra and The Swing Septet. He met and became friends with many world-famous jazz guitarists, including Django Reinhardt, Carmen Mastren, Les Paul, Mundell Lowe, Barney Kessel, Herb Ellis, Kenny Burrell, Tal Farlow, George Benson, Jimmy Raney, George Barnes, Wes Montgomery, Joe Pass, Charlie Byrd, Laurindo Almeida, Jack Marshall, Pat Martino, Pat Metheny, Tommy Tedesco and George Van Eps. After seeing *Moto Perpetuo For Guitar*, which Ivor dedicated to George, Van Eps wrote, 'Dear Ivor, I am very proud of the dedication in your new book and I thank you, for I have not experienced an honour like this before from a very talented player/writer such as yourself.'

Like each of the masters listed above, Ivor's enthusiasm for the jazz guitar was always on the boil, encouraging him to set down in this book his favourite examples of those jazz guitarists whose genius inspired him to maintain his enthusiasm for the instrument. He died in 1998.

CONTENTS

PREFACE

The time around my 80th birthday coincided with a series of events which, though unconnected, acted together as a catalyst: the second book of my selections of famous jazz-guitar solos was published; Bucky Pizzarelli and his son, John, played an entertaining programme of guitar duets at London's Pizza On The Park, which I reviewed for *Guitarist* magazine; and jazz lover Tony Harrison threw a birthday party for me, where I met a keen young guitarist who had never heard of most of the finest jazz players, including Charlie Christian, Barney Kessel, Herb Ellis, Tal Farlow, Wes Montgomery, Joe Pass and Bucky Pizzarelli, who was present at the party.

These events came together when I visited the British Music Fair, where my book *Famous Jazz Guitar Solos (Book II)* was newly displayed. At the stand of *Guitarist* magazine (published by Music Maker Publications), I proudly showed a copy to the chairman of the company, Terry Day, who promptly commissioned me to write a book on a subject of my choice.

It then occurred to me that generations of musicians had grown up since the days of the above-mentioned jazz guitarists, and that they must surely want to know more about them and their music.

The result is this representation of outstanding players (in some historical order), their solos and analyses of their styles, together with potted biographies. Clearly a limit had to be set and a choice made, or the project could have been endless. I have therefore concentrated on innovators, rather than merely great players, and if the reader disagrees with my choice then all I can say is that such matters must, to some extent, be personal.

My aim is to introduce – or reintroduce – these great performers to the eyes and ears of both experienced musicians who have long admired them and to the younger players who have never heard of them.

Ivor Mairants
September 1992

FOREWORDS

Reading through Ivor Mairants' marvellous book is, for me, a bit like examining a family tree – my own. It brings up feelings of nostalgia for the past, contentment about the present and a tremendous excitement concerning what is to come. With a lineage like the one so beautifully detailed here, the future seems bright indeed.

Many of these guitarists I never saw play, but with the blessing of electronic recordings they are present for me, like pictures of a relative I never knew. How fortunate to have this lovingly detailed and organised book, this record of the family tree of jazz guitar. Thank you, Ivor.

Jim Hall
21 May 1993

In my opinion, there was no better authority than Ivor Mairants to write the definitive story on the subject of the great jazz guitarists. Readers of this excellent volume will find that Ivor was equally at home in the fields of jazz and classical music, and he regularly indulged in the art when playing with leading British orchestras on television, radio, in concert halls and in recording studios, and the many 'greats' with whom he was personally acquainted hold him in very high esteem, as both a friend and a mentor. Who better, then, to provide this wealth of reading pleasures for our enjoyment?

Robert Farnon
June 1993

I first met Ivor when I was a mere jazz sapling at twelve years old. I had gone up to London to buy a guitar, having saved up £100 from doing gigs with my dad, and I needed someone to guide me towards the right instrument that day when providence directed me to Ivor's shop in Rathbone Place. Ivor told me that he had just the guitar for me and, thanks to him, I left the shop with a Guild Starfire in my hands, the first really good instrument I had ever owned. That was to be the start of a lifelong friendship which saw our paths cross on many occasions, with Ivor and his wife, Lily, always taking great and courteous interest at every development in my career as a musician. *The Great Jazz Guitarists* is representative of the life's work of a kind, generous and very special man. I know how much the writing of this tremendous book meant to Ivor and I'm honoured to be included in its pages and delighted to have been given the chance to write the introduction to this new edition.

Martin Taylor
Autumn 2001

PART 1

THE GREAT JAZZ AGE

INTRODUCTION

I discovered the guitar through the recordings of Eddie Lang and the great jazz instrumentalists of the '20s and '30s. Listening today to their spontaneous improvisations and extemporaneous artistry demonstrates how their sparkle hasn't diminished and proves, in the words of Duke Ellington (whose band was a prime example of improvisational jazz-ensemble playing), that 'T'ain't what you do, it's the way that you do it – that's what brings results.'

In arithmetic, the correct computation of a multiplication sum is sufficient, but simply playing the correct notes doesn't result in a musical performance. The following pages of transcribed improvisations may be a correctly written record of the notes played by the various guitarists, but no matter how accurately they are transcribed they won't sound like jazz when performed, unless the player 'lifts' the phrases off the manuscript and sends them bouncing along the airwaves.

Over the years, I've had the good fortune to hear many of the great jazz guitarists, and in this book and its companion volume I have attempted to provide a selection of what are, in my estimation, their most memorable solos, inventions that have made a lasting impression on 20th-century guitar playing.

Even though we're limited to the two-dimensional written notation of the printed page, a third dimension, sound, is possible with the help of recordings (where available) and live performances (when possible). Don't limit your listening to jazz guitarists; lend an ear to all great instrumentalists and jazz groups, compare their styles and try to analyse their personal differences of phrasing and expression.

When I pointed out in a BBC broadcast the changes of style and gradual development of phrasing in the playing of the early jazz pioneers – including Joe 'King' Oliver, Louis Armstrong, Bix Beiderbecke, Frankie Trumbauer, Jimmy Dorsey, Earl Hines and the contrapuntal genius of Eddie Lang – listeners commented that they had been unaware of these features. They were delighted to have been enlightened, as I hope you will be, with the first guitar transcriptions in the First Jazz Age.

1 EDDIE LANG

'Stringin' The Blues' (Venuti and Lang)'
'Singin' The Blues 'Til My Daddy Comes Home' (Conrad and Robinson)
'I'm Coming, Virginia' (Heyward and Cook)
'Someday Sweetheart' (Spikes)
'Three Blind Mice' (Trumbauer and Moorhouse)
'In De Ruff' (Venuti and Lang)

Eddie Lang (real name Salvatore Massaro) was born in Philadelphia on 25 October 1902 and died on 26 March 1933. His father was a guitar maker when he lived in Italy, and he built Salvatore a 'cigar-box' guitar when he was a very small boy. At school, young Salvatore learned to play the violin alongside his classmate and lifelong friend Joe Venuti, the great jazz violinist.

Then Salvatore changed his name to Eddie Lang and, at the age of 22, joined The Mound City Blue Blowers on banjo witha view to becoming a professional musician. In 1926, The Blue Blowers visited London and played an engagement at the Piccadilly Hotel, but when they returned to the US they dispensed with Eddie's services and hired a guitar player instead. It was then that Eddie took up the guitar and began to record with his chum Joe Venuti. Their first recording was 'Stringin' The Blues', the first of Eddie's pieces that I've selected for inclusion here.

At first, Eddie played a Martin flat-top guitar, but after the development of the arch-top f-hole guitar he changed to a a model with a round hole before later switching to a Gibson L5. In the 1870s, Orville Gibson modelled his guitar to the same principles employed for the construction of the mandolin – that is, a carved top and back, similar to a violin. By the time Gibson died, in 1918, the Gibson Mandolin Manufacturing Company was well established, making carved-top guitars for use in dance bands. In 1920, Lloyd Loar, a well-known mandolin and stringed-instrument player, composer and acoustic engineer joined Gibson and developed new innovations, including the two-footed adjustable bridge, the f-holes, the raised fingerplate and adjustable trussrod. These developments elevated the Gibson guitar to its highest level, culminating in the L5.

Eddie Lang became famous for using an L5, and where he led, the guitar fraternity followed. Between the recording of 'Stringin' The Blues' in 1926 and his early death in 1933, Eddie had become the strongest influence on both individual jazz guitarists and dance bands. In fact, his sphere of influence extended to include musicians on both sides of the Atlantic, as proved by the *Melody Maker* readers' poll of 1937, in which he polled 1,737 votes, the highest number recorded for any instrument, despite having been dead for four years.

During his brief career, Eddie recorded with Red Nichols and his Five Pennies, Joe Venuti, Lonnie Johnson, Bix Beiderbecke and Bessie Smith, and was in constant demand for recording work. In 1929, he and Joe Venuti joined Paul Whiteman's band and went to California to be featured in the film *The King Of Jazz*. Lang then became Bing Crosby's accompanist, and was reputed to be earning $1,000 a week when he died on 26 March 1933 due to complications after a tonsillectomy.

Any guitarist wishing to play the first transcription here, 'Stringin' The Blues', must first consider the style of the period, when the main aim of the guitar was to produce as big an acoustic tone as the instrument could project. Despite having to play a string action much higher than today's and with heavy strings (or perhaps because of these impediments), Eddie Lang was without question the master of producing a good tone with full volume. He was also a master of producing 'blue' notes, bending strings and using a healthy vibrato when required.

The piece itself exemplifies the early Lang style and contains a number of his best-known phrases. The introduction is in a simple music-hall style, but can be phrased in a stylish way. The first eight bars should be played fully and rhythmically, and although the melodic line is very simple, built on a four-bar harmonic sequence (tonic/tonic/dominant seventh/tonic), the diminished chord at the end of each second bar in the four-bar group saves the sequence from banality, as do the G and D in the fourth bar and the variation in the melody of the second four bars.

Although the second eight bars contain the same harmony as the first eight, there are subtle developments in the melody line, both in the pitch of the line and because of the injection of bends (ie blue notes). Make the most of them.

In section (C), there is a change of key and a complete change of melody, with a long bend in the third bar in which the B♯ must be held for a whole beat before the string is bent up a semitone to C♯. The fifth bar begins after a quaver rest and again changes the feel while retaining the form. Harmonically, it is dominant to tonic instead of the other way around.

Section (D) acts as a kind of middle-eight or release. It also reverts to the original key and progression while altering the melodic effects.

Section (G) goes off on a tangent, both in key and in phrasing, although without straying too far. In fact, it prepares the ear for a recapitulation of the first section, despite a completely different set of harmonies and melodies. Breaks were very popular in this era, and Lang uses single-note runs, harmonics and double-stopping to produce surprise effects.

In (H), the phrasing is again varied by resting the melody on the first beat of every two bars, making a false finish at the end of eight bars and repeating the four-bar harmony a minor third below, thereby leading us into the last section, again in the key of E. The melody of the second four bars is also repeated a major sixth higher.

From section (J), the piece takes on a new rhythmic and harmonic shape. It becomes a lively 32-bar composition with a two-bar tag in the shape of a one-bar repeat of the third and fourth bars from the end.

Overall, the piece packs many surprises and, considering that it was recorded on 8 November 1926, a great deal of originality as well.

'Stringin' The Blues' is followed by 'Singin' The Blues 'Til My Daddy Comes Home', which illustrates Eddie Lang's great talent as a member of the rhythm section. He laid down a strong rhythm as well as accompaniment, and in addition wove a musical counter-melody.

For the third piece, I've selected 'I'm Coming, Virginia', recorded in 1927 and set out here in the form of a two-part reduction of the band arrangement. The purpose is to illustrate the style of the other great jazz musicians who worked with Lang and with whom he made many recordings, each player being influenced by the others.

It also demonstrates how the guitar was integrated into the arrangement, first in the introduction and then as the accompaniment to Bix's melodic jazz solo. The guitar then invents a rather modernistic bridge passage, which modulates to the verse in the minor key. Near the end, the guitar has a solo triplet break before the first solo arpeggio.

Eddie Lang was strongly influenced by other musical companions besides his close friend Joe Venuti. He was influenced most of all, in my opinion, by the great blues guitarist Lonnie Johnson, with whom he often recorded

under the pseudonym Blind Willie Dunn. In fact, the intermingling of their two styles became the basis of jazz-guitar phrasing for years to come and strongly influenced the generations of guitarists that followed Lang.

After Eddie's early death in 1933, the jazz-guitar leadership was continued by a group of guitarists who had come to the guitar from the banjo (as did Lang) but who adopted a lighter string action and a more bouncy style of phrasing, using a chordal conception rather than a single-string solo style. This group of players was led at first by Dick McDonough and his friend Carl Kress, who recorded the famous duets 'Stagefright' and 'Chicken À La Swing', as well as George Van Eps and his pupil Allan Reuss. (McDonough, Van Eps and Reuss all played in Benny Goodman's band at one time.) However, in spite of the changing styles provided by this famous quartet, the Eddie Lang/Lonnie Johnson phrases found their way into the music of their successors, for Lang and Johnson had laid down a lasting foundation.

In my notes on 'I'm Coming, Virginia', I mentioned the importance of influences and the way in which Eddie Lang was influenced by the great jazz players of the period. One can also be influenced by unstylish players, and the clarinettist Boyd Senter was such an influence. Why, then, have I transcribed Lang's guitar solo on Boyd Senter's recording of 'Someday Sweetheart'? Well, it was the first record that I ever heard of Lang's, and the one that made me throw away my banjo and buy a guitar, which may prove that, no matter how poor a solo a great master performs, the tone and feeling somehow still penetrate the dross and affect the eager listener.

The first eight bars of the solo are played by Lang as an introduction to the main event, but after a verse and a chorus of clarinet Lang uses almost the same notes as he did in the introductory first eight bars of his 24-bar solo (a very simple one). No doubt the bumbling undertow of Senter's clarinet put Lang off extending himself. I don't know why Lang sank this low for companionship. I'm sure it wasn't for the session money.

'Three Blind Mice' is a simple theme but played with great charm. Lang produces a lot of punch by pushing along after quavers – or 'backbeats', as they were sometimes called – in bar three.

From the ninth bar, he employs the simple device of picking two strings together on the same fret positions to create fourths on strings one and two and thirds on strings two and three. Then, In order to build up to the end of the solo, he employs an ascending/ descending bend in bars 14 and 15, but in bar 14 the bend is in quavers and the one in bar 15 is a quaver, crotchet and crotchet, in a backbeat. Very effective.

The two choruses of blues taken from 'In De Ruff' show Lang off in an entirely different way. Here is the Lonnie Johnson loose, limpid style. The left-hand fingering throughout is very important and essential to the sound of the wail. Sustain the sound for as long as possible in the first chorus and make it lie back. The slurs must be continuous, unbroken and clear. It's not as easy as it looks. Use great pressure.

The second chorus is more tricky, and each two-bar phrase must be clean, slick and played in one breath. When each two-bar phrase is mastered, they should then be joined together and sound without a break.

The slurred triplets that were first heard from Lang and Johnson are still the stock in trade of guitar phrasing and should be perfected, until they can be played without having to think about it. Listen to some of the later guitar solos and remember how many times they are still being used in jazz, rock and any other style of guitar playing. Not only was Lang influenced by Johnson, but so were Teddy Bunn and, perhaps, Eddie Durham.

Stringin' The Blues (Venuti and Lang)

Recorded November 1926 and released on OKEH 914D, COE 4454 DB 5001 Matrix 142697 (Columbia C21-24). Joe Venuti and Eddie Lang.

Singin' The Blues 'Til My Daddy Comes Home (Conrad and Robinson)

Recorded on 4 February 1927, New York. First issued on OKEH 40772. Eddie Lang with The Frankie Trumbauer Orchestra: Frankie Trumbauer (C melody sax), Bix Beiderbecke, Jimmy Dorsey (clarinet), Chauncey Moorehouse (drums), Bill Rank (trombone) and Itzy Riskin (piano).

I'm Coming, Virginia (Heyward and Cook)

Recorded in 1927 and released on OKEH 40843 (81083). Eddie Lang with The Frankie Trumbauer Orchestra with Bix Beiderbecke (cornet).

Someday Sweetheart (Spikes)

Released on Parlophone R3351 W80325A. Boyd Senter (clarinet and piano) and Eddie Lang (guitar).

Three Blind Mice (Trumbauer and Moorehouse)

Released on Parlophone R105 (S1273). The Frankie Trumbauer Orchestra with Bix Beiderbecke, Lang, Rollini, Schutt and Venuti. Guitar solo by Eddie Lang.

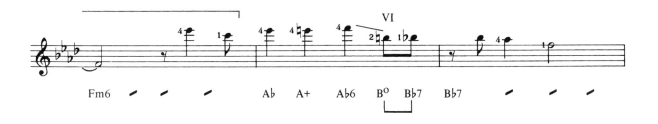

In De Ruff (Venuti and Lang)

Released on Columbia RB686 (W265149). Joe Venuti and his Blue Six, with Eddie Lang (guitar).

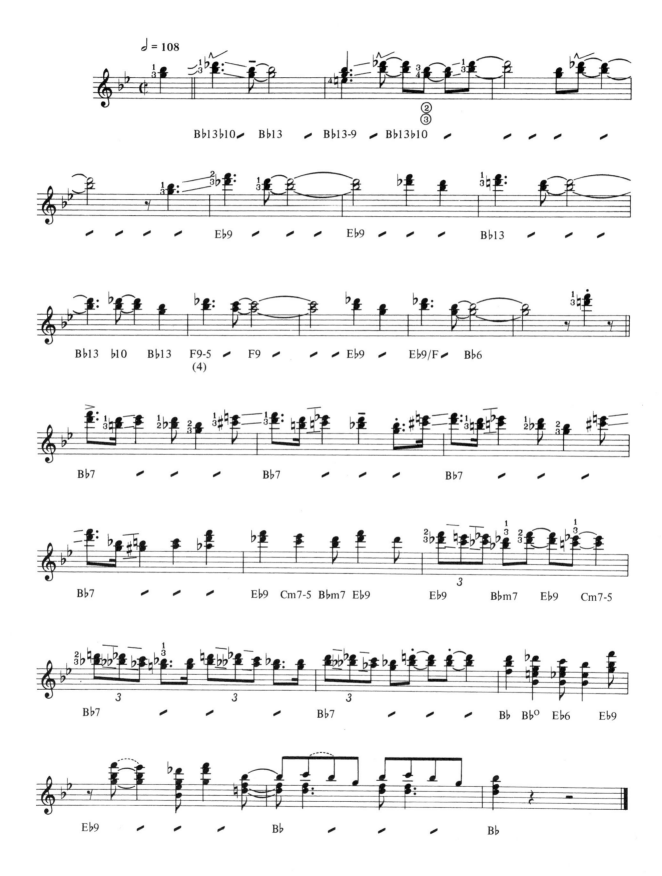

2 LONNIE JOHNSON

'Paducah' (Warren and Robin)
'Deep Minor Rhythm Stomp' (Johnson and Lang)

In 'Paducah', Lonnie Johnson (born February 1889, New Orleans, died 16 June 1970) takes 24 bars on his twelve-string guitar. Recorded under the direction of saxophonist/arranger Don Redman, one hears a much lighter touch and easier bounce than in Lang's playing in general, except on 'In De Ruff', which is distinctly similar, both in the singing tone and the triplets in thirds.

I've written the eighth notes here intentionally as dotted quavers and semiquavers, although they actually sound like the first and last notes of a triplet. However, the phrases really swing lightly. Take care to play in the positions marked in order to make the phrases flow. Although players have their own ways of fingering, the fingering marked here will produce the best lilt.

The second chorus commences with a triplet lead-in, slurring into the 13th bar and continuing the triplets with downstrokes. Make a little *crescendo* to the middle of the 14th bar and then a slight *diminuendo* on the descending thirds before building up again.

In the 17th bar, articulate the Cs as you would a bass note and syncopate the bar accordingly. Continue unabated, with much animation, until you come to a climax at the E♭ diminished chord at the beginning of the 22nd bar. Slur down to the C diminished chord and finish in swinging style with the string bend from F to F♯ before finishing on the E♭ tonic in bar 23. Then build up, almost repeating the phrase, to the final E flats in the 24th bar. Play without hesitation.

It's often been asked why a piece in the key of D major is entitled 'Deep Minor Rhythm Stomp'. If one listens carefully, one may realise that there is really no contradiction. The piece was recorded in the very early days of jazz and, because of the many blues or minor nuances which occur, it was quite a natural blues phenomenon to use F naturals slurred up from E or F naturals bent up to F♯, or from F♯ to F, whereby the string is released after being bent up to F♯.

The chord of B♭7 following the chord of D major also adds to the minor effect. This is an effect used, for example, in the blues tune 'St James' Infirmary' (ie B♭7, A7, Dm), and it's the sound effect, more than the key signature, that hits the ear.

The ear is also immediately affected by the strong, bouncy attack used by the two players, both in the melody and in the accompaniment. The playing is hard-hitting, free from any rhythmic inhibitions, and provides a perfect basis of jazz blues played on the guitar.

The solo contains the fundamental blues lick, performed with feeling, freedom and fluency, while the rhythm accompaniment contains the basis of the tight, rhythmic offbeat, coupled with moving bass notes and connecting chords. In fact, it's a way of playing rhythm that formed the ground rules for future players. The same may also be said of the solo phrasing, despite the lack of sophistication, compared to the blues bending of the '80s and '90s. Many an Eric Clapton phrase can be traced back to Lonnie Johnson. Johnson also has the knack of altering every repetitive phrase by using a different inflection, or a slight note change – a sign of good composition. It's because of these slight changes that I've carefully marked each inflection the way it is, rather than just describing it as a bend and letting it go at that. And it's important to note that a slur is not just a slide; a hammer-on or -off is not a portamento; an upbend that becomes a sustained upper semitone (ie F♮ to F♯) is not the same as a bend that falls back to the original note (ie F♮ to F♯ and then back to F♮).

Compare the more sophisticated bending and sustaining effects of Eric Clapton, BB King or Sister Rosetta Tharpe with those of Lonnie Johnson and you'll find that the ties haven't been severed. This is why I consider 'Deep Minor Rhythm Stomp' (and the word 'stomp' in this title means literally a stomping beat) to be such an important example of guitar blues.

Paducah (Warren and Robin)

Recorded 13 October 1928, New York. Released on CBS 81836, *50 Years Of Jazz Guitar*. Original OKEH 8627 (MXW401218-B). Lonnie Johnson (guitar) with The Chocolate Dandies.

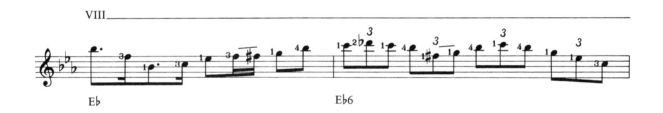

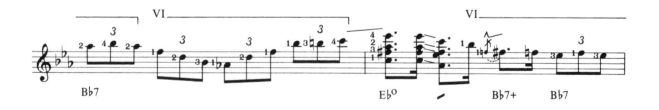

Deep Minor Rhythm Stomp (Johnson and Lang)

Recorded 9 October 1929, New York. Released on OKEH MXW403039A under the names of Blind Willie Dunn (Eddie Lang, playing rhythm throughout on acoustic guitar) and Lonnie Johnson (playing solo on a twelve-string guitar).

3 THE SECOND GUITAR SCHOOL

Dick McDonough, Carl Kress, George Van Eps, Allan Reuss
and the post-Eddie Lang change of guitar style

As already mentioned, when he was playing as Bing Crosby's accompanist, Eddie Lang began to suffer from a chronically inflamed throat, and Bing – who had become a close friend – was very concerned for his health and therefore advised him to see a doctor, who in turn advised a tonsillectomy. Unfortunately, during the operation, while Lang was under general anaesthetic, a blood clot developed and he never regained consciousness, and the world was deprived of a guitarist whose full, round tone on the f-hole arch-top guitar and whose brilliant contrapuntal accompaniments have never been equalled. Nevertheless, his musical influences are still evident today, although in a modified way.

After Eddie Lang, the stage was set for a change in guitar style, from Lang's heavily strung, high string action and hard-attack picking tone to the lighter, lower-strung string action and smoother, more lyrical style initiated by Dick McDonough and his contemporaries Carl Kress, George Van Eps and Allan Reuss. However, it's difficult to separate McDonough and Van Eps during this period (1934–5) since their lives were somewhat interentwined for a short but rather important while.

Before this time, Dick McDonough (born 1904, died 1938) and Carl Kress (born 1907, died 1965) were both engaged in recording with a number of dance orchestras and becoming very well known among guitarists outside the USA. In the meantime, McDonough was also recording with Don Voorhees, leader of the house orchestra at Columbia Studios, playing on banjo and tenor guitar, and was working with the famous Smith Bellew Orchestra. Later, in 1933, he joined Benny Goodman's Orchestra for a while and made a number of recordings with him.

Meanwhile, George Van Eps (born in 1913) came from a very musical family. His father, Fred Van Eps, was one of the world's greatest banjoists and toured nationwide as a solo act with piano accompaniment. During the period 1913–18, his accompanist was the great George Gershwin. Naturally, little George (Van Eps) saw a good deal of big

George (Gershwin) and had many opportunities to soak up Gershwin's rich harmonic piano style. George Van Eps became a good banjo player, but he found that the rich harmonies of Gershwin were inaccessible on the banjo. This weakness was remedied in 1924, when Roger Wolfe Kahn and his fabulous orchestra, featuring Joe Venuti and Eddie Lang, appeared in New York. George was so enraptured by Lang's guitar playing that he immediately wanted to play the guitar instead of the banjo. Soon enough, he met Lang, who, on seeing the boy's keenness, handed him his guitar. It was tuned the conventional way (unlike others around at the time that were tuned like banjos), but Van Eps didn't find this an obstacle and fell in love with the instrument. In fact, Eddie eventually lent George a guitar.

But Fred Van Eps wasn't convinced and withheld his support until 1928, when they both went to hear André Segovia at his New York debut. At this time, George began to play in earnest, and in the ensuing years he became very friendly with Dick McDonough and was invited to share a flat with him in West 76th Street, New York.

One day, as George told me during his 1986 tour of England with 'Peanuts' Hucko, Dick told George that he had decided to join an orchestra that was being formed for a sensational new theatre production that was to be known as The 9.15 Revue. The show would be 'broken in' in Boston before opening in New York, and he had recommended George to the guitar chair of The Smith Bellew Orchestra. George was delighted, of course, and it proved to be his first big break with a famous band. The 9.15 Revue, unfortunately, folded after a fortnight and never did reach Broadway, but when Dick returned to New York he told George that he had no desire to return to The Smith Bellew Orchestra. Even so, the two remained friends, often alternating on recordings with Paul Whiteman's Orchestra and on other sessions.

In 1933, Dick joined Benny Goodman's band and recorded a number of titles with him, his name appearing in the personnel list of 'Love Me Or Leave Me' (according to the 1938 edition of Charles Delaunay's *Hot Discography*), in which the middle-eight bars comprise a guitar solo that sounds like George Van Eps. Perhaps I'm not mistaken, either, as George may have deputised for Dick at that session. After all, George joined Goodman in 1934, before he joined forces with Ray Noble in 1935. When I spoke to George about the solo in 'Love Me Or Leave Me', he couldn't remember whether he'd played it or not, which shows how closely their styles resembled each other's at the time.

Dick McDonough also died young, collapsing while in the studio in 1938, and so another brilliant guitarist was lost, although not before leaving the legacy of his guitar duets with Carl Kress.

The fourth guitar player to become a prolific recording man was Allan Reuss (born 1915, died 1988), who had studied with George Van Eps and later also joined Benny Goodman's band, where he stayed for about four years before going to Hollywood. He played in the same chordal style employed by the other three, illustrated by his solo in 'If I Could Be With You'.

Van Eps joined Ray Noble in Hollywood, having had a new seven-string neck fitted to his Epiphone guitar, the seventh string being an A tuned an octave lower than the fifth string. First, however, a short example of Dick McDonough's innovation using a lower string action and lighter strings in the following example from 'By Heck' with The Dorsey Brothers Band.

4 DICK McDONOUGH

'By Heck' (Henry)
'Honeysuckle Rose' (Waller and Razaf)

'By Heck' was the record on which I first heard Dick McDonough play, and at the time his performance was startling and novel, especially the sound of his guitar, which was much lighter and gentler than Lang's and smoother, rhythmically. One wasn't aware of the plectrum hitting the strings on impact, as when Lang played. All of this, of course, was due to the lower action and the use of lighter-gauge strings.

The first part of the music features a 'crushed-note' effect (ie the effect produced by simultaneously playing two notes semitones apart on two adjacent strings), and the second solo section was constructed by using a minor chord (arpeggiated) with a melody note in the bass, first descending and then returning to its original tonic position. In this instance, the chord is B minor, and the melodic descent commences on B, then moves down in semitones as far as F♯ and before moving up again. The other interesting effect of this movement is that, for six bars, it's used as an accompaniment to a muted trumpet solo, and then, after a two-bar guitar break reintroducing the crushed notes, the guitar continues by playing the previous six bars again, this time without the trumpet. The originality of it all hit me unforgettably, and no doubt McDonough's ingenuity had the same effect on the New York jazz fraternity, who considered him the best jazz guitarist in town.

Looking now at 'Honeysuckle Rose', after the meditative introduction, the first two choruses are given a bouncy rhythm and a firm touch, with subtle changes in melody and harmony here and there. For example, there's a slight change of melody in bar four and a fill-in figure from bar five to bar six that is similar to the trombone part. In the eighth bar, instead of E7 to A7 we have a nice melody on the chords of E13–9/A13 and A♭9, leading to the Am7/A13 in the ninth bar – rather daring for the period.

In bars 15–16, McDonough performs a characteristic break in arpeggiated tenths leading to the middle-eight bars, which in their simplest form comprise two bars each of D7, G7, E7 and A7, becoming half a bar each of | D7 Dm7 | G♯ D7 | played in arpeggio form. This figure is something that McDonough made his own, and was often copied by other guitarists. The two bars before (C) also provide a typical McDonough phrase, while at (E) (the middle of the second chorus) octaves are used to good effect, and at two bars before (F) another interesting break ensues.

At the end of the second chorus, there is a slight retard to a half-chorus at a slower tempo before returning to the original speed of ♪ = 84 for the reprise, ending with almost the same figure as it began with. It could be said that, in this arrangement of 'Honeysuckle Rose', McDonough produces a fair demonstration of the jazz-guitar style of the '30s, which he initiated.

By Heck (Henry)

Modern Rhythm series 180 (1.13449) 01575B. The Dorsey Brothers Orchestra with Dick McDonough.

Honeysuckle Rose (Waller and Razaf)

Recorded 22 November 1934, New York. ARC Test Recorded (MXTO1483-1) and on CBS 81826 1976, *50 Years Of Jazz Guitar*. Guitar solo by Dick McDonough.

5 GEORGE VAN EPS

'Love Me Or Leave Me' (Donaldson and Kahn)

In 1939, George Van Eps (born 7 August 1913, Plainfield, New Jersey, died 1998) was playing a guitar manufactured by Epiphone Inc, who at the time wanted to extend the range of the guitar. At first, Van Eps experimented by removing the first E string, substituting a second B and tuning all of the other strings down a fourth, before eventually deciding to retain the normal tuning of the six strings and adding a seventh, made especially for him by John D'Addario, whose company still provides the low A strings.

The guitar was delivered to Van Eps during 1938, and he soon moved to Hollywood to join Ray Noble, with whom he'd been recording in New York. Meanwhile, he'd written a guitar tutor, which formed the basis of his *Harmonic Mechanisms For The Guitar*, as well as a folio of guitar solos.

It was at this time that Epiphone published his 'Study In Eighths'. Although not reproduced here, it demonstrates well Van Eps' style, particularly his chordal and arpeggio playing, which in turn is obviously influenced by the arpeggio style played by Dick McDonough in 'By Heck'. In this piece, he takes a popular four-bar interlude and develops it into an original-sounding phrase, then goes on to further develop this sequence for the next twelve bars before returning to the beginning. Take a look at the following chord changes:

|| Em / Em maj7 / Em7 | A9 / A13 / A9 / A13 | A7+5 / B7+5 (♯9) / Em/A7 | G / B7+5 / B7 | Em / Em maj7 / Em7 | Em7 / F♯m7 / B7–9 | Em / Em maj7 / Em7 | Em7 / Am 7/9 / Am7 | Em7 / / / | A11/13 / A9 / | Am7 / / / | B9 / / / ||

Clearly, the second four bars are a variation of the first four, but bars nine to twelve act as a bridge passage before returning to the original phrase at the beginning six bars and coming to a conclusion at the coda. The ending is in the relative key of G major and the chord symbols are as follows:

Bar 1　　　　　　Bar 2　Bar 3
|| G / A13 / D7 (+5–9) / D13 / D7+5 / D13 | G6 | G6 ||

The piece listed here is the eight-bar guitar solo in 'Love Me Or Leave Me'. The solo of this piece has generally been considered (by guitarists) to be the best part of the arrangement and has always been accepted as having been played by George Van Eps. However, as I mentioned earlier, doubt has been cast on this assumption by the entry in Charles Delaunay's *Hot Discography*, which lists Dick McDonough in the guitar chair. I can only presume that, although McDonough's name was in the company's books, Van Eps sat in for him on that particular date.

The chordal solo is played with punch and in a moving rhythm, involving chordal changes along the fingerboard to ensure smooth shifts, and either guitarist could have played it. But semitone changes going up from B♭7 to B13 and back, in bars five and six, seem to stamp it as Van Eps, particularly the triplet lead-in of F, G and A into the B13 chord at the end of bar five into bar six. The last two bars must also have sounded pretty ingenious at the time.

The third piece, 'I Never Knew That Roses Grew', was recorded on 1 August 1956 and released on Columbia on the album *Mellow Guitar* (CL929). The album was recorded in Hollywood with amplified guitar, accompanied by bass and drums, and the session took place during a very fruitful professional period in which Van Eps was playing for Paul Weston and his orchestra, as well as having other prolific studio work in Hollywood.

From the very beginning of the six-bar introduction, the piece teems with originality, particularly in the last two bars:

| D / G / | Em7 / A13 |

Clear and uncluttered. The first few bars of the chorus introduce the straight melody...almost. From the three-quaver lead-in to the fifth and sixth bars, inclusive, the whole harmonic structure is enhanced by a chromatic chord that is used both in passing and as a suspension (D♯m to Em; E♯m to Em6) leading to the tonic chord in the seventh bar.

The tonic, D, then moves up a semitone to E♭ in the second half of the bar, enabling the eighth bar to be transformed to a B♭7 (ie the dominant of E♭) before descending back to D♮ via a chord of A9+ with a B♭ melody (A9+−9) – ie A, G, B♮, F♮, B♭.

Bars nine to twelve, although not really chromatic, produce a variation in the melody aided by the B♭ in the chord of Gm against the sixth, E, and the major seventh, F♯. The melody then bounces onto the 16th bar, which modulates to the middle section via the chord of C♯7 to F♯m in the 17th bar.

The middle section is just as intriguing. Although uncluttered and uncomplicated, it is absolutely melodic to the syncopated 23rd bar, leading back to the last eight-bar phrase.

To take apart the whole arrangement requires more space than I have allocated here, but if you can get hold of a recording or sheet music, look at bar 26, where a lead-in of four 16th notes is used as a springboard to the 27th bar. All in all, 'I Never Knew That Roses Grew' is a study of sufficient depth to enable the student to give a fair performance in a springy tempo and to teach the player a great deal of the Van Eps musical *modus vivendi*. I highly recommend it.

Love Me Or Leave Me (Donaldson and Kahn)

Recorded with Benny Goodman and his Orchestra. Released on HMV B8504, Swing Music series 88, 1936. Arranger: Dean Kincade.

6 CARL KRESS

'S' Wonderful' (Gershwin)

Carl Kress (born 20 October 1907, Newark, New Jersey, died 10 June 1965, Reno, Nevada) began his musical career on the banjo before later turning to the guitar, although it was the early banjo influence that led him to experiment with alternative tunings on the guitar.

In 1932, he briefly recorded two duets with the great Eddie Lang, the historic 'Feelin' My Way' and 'Pickin' My Way', which established him as a superb accompanist. He was in great demand as a rhythm guitarist with the famous bands of the day – those led by Paul Whiteman, Frankie Trumbauer, Bix Beiderbecke and Red Nichols – and played with the original Dorsey Brothers Band.

In 1934, he joined Dick McDonough in the recording of the original duets 'Stagefright' and 'Danzon'. Among Kress' compositions was 'Peg-Leg Shuffle', dedicated to a dancer who dragged one leg. In order to imitate the effect on the guitar, he scraped the pick along a bass string, thereby producing a swishing sound.

After experimenting with various tunings, he settled on B♭, F, D, G, A and D, as illustrated here:

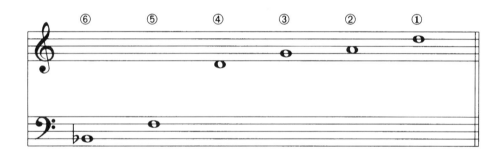

In 1951, Kress was the resident guitarist on *The Gerry Moore Show* in New York. During a performance, Moore spotted George Barnes in the audience and introduced him. Turning to Carl Kress, he said, 'You two fellows should get together.' The guitarists did meet, and became good friends, but it wasn't until 1961, ten years later, that they became the first permanent guitar duo working together. They made a number of albums and played some notable engagements, including the New York Town Hall and the White House (for President Lyndon B Johnson), and while I was in New York in 1964 they appeared at Birdland, on Broadway. In 1962, they teamed up with Bud Freeman to record a delicious album for which George Barnes wrote the title tune, 'Something Tender'.

Carl Kress and George Barnes worked together until 1965, when Carl died while still in his prime as a talented guitarist, unique in his field.

Kress was undoubtedly better known for his full, round tone and firm accompanying skill than for his solo playing, so it's refreshing to hear this master chordist in a 32-bar solo of his own, taken from 'S' Wonderful'. The piece is played at a fast swing tempo and Kress adds life and zest with his clean execution and firm, syncopated chordal rhythms in an exhilarating performance. Although it's highly enjoyable to listen to, there's little improvisational content, compared to the work of his contemporaries McDonough, Van Eps or Reuss. But, as we can hear from his duet performances with Eddie Lang, Dick McDonough and, later, George Barnes, as an accompanist or as a strong back-up player, he was the right man for the job.

S' Wonderful (Gershwin)

Recorded 27 April 1956. Released on Brunswick 7663 (MXB19116). Frankie Trumbauer and his orchestra: Ed Wade, Charlie Teagarden (trumpets), Jack Teagarden (trombone), Artie Shaw (clarinet), Joe Cordaro (clarinet, alto sax), Frankie Trumbauer (C melody sax), Mutt Hayes (tenor sax), Roy Bargy (piano), Carl Kress (guitar), Artie Miller (bass) and Stan King (drums). Guitar solo by Carl Kress.

Ab6 Abmaj7 Bb7 Eb6/9

Eb6/9 D7-9 G Gmaj7

G6 Bm D9 G7

C13 F13 F9+5 Bb9

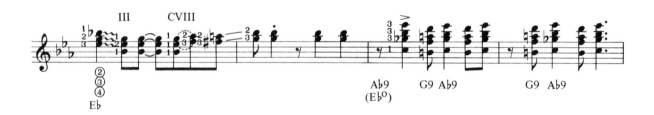

III CVIII Ab9 (Eb⁰) G9 Ab9 G9 Ab9 Eb

Fm7 Bb13 Trombone Eb Bb7

7 ALLAN REUSS

'If I Could Be With You One Hour Tonight' (Creamer and Johnson)

If ever a disciple's guitar style resembles his master's, it's that of Allan Reuss (born 15 June 1915, New York City, died 4 June 1988). Four years Van Eps' junior, Reuss played the banjo from the age of twelve and then, in 1934, discovered a strong desire to play the guitar and took lessons from George Van Eps. Six months later, when George vacated the guitar chair in The Benny Goodman Band, Allan filled it to Goodman's satisfaction, staying with him for four years. He was also an immensely popular session guitarist, recording on the Vocalion label for Teddy Wilson, Harry James, Helen Ward and also the legendary Billie Holiday.

In the '40s, he too went to Hollywood, and until 1976 he was occupied with his Los Angeles studio dates.

However, when his wife became ill, he retired from playing and sold his instruments in order to care for her. She died in January 1979, and he told me that he would never play again. And so, apart from Van Eps, who is still going strong, no one is left of the famous foursome.

A study of 'If I Could Be With You' shows the powerful influence that the three older players had on Reuss, particularly in bars nine and ten, where he ascends from E♭m7 to Emaj7 before returning, via A♭13.

It's remarkable how this piano style lasted for more than an era and only gradually faded out with the advent of the electric guitar. But in the '80s, a number of players, including Joe Pass and Tal Farlow, have included chordal solos in their repertoires.

If I Could Be With You One Hour Tonight (Creamer and Johnson)

Recorded 1935 and released on HMV B8480. Allan Reuss with The Benny Goodman Band.

8 TEDDY BUNN

'I've Got The World On A String' (Arlen and Koehler)
'Way Down Yonder In New Orleans' (Creamer and Layton)
'Four Or Five Times' (Byron)

It's more than 50 years since I first heard the deep, happy, lightly rhythmic and creatively original improvisations of Theodore Leroy (Teddy) Bunn (born 1909, died 1978). It would be an understatement to say that he was under-rated and under-published, especially compared to Eddie Lang or Charlie Christian, and he has also been completely overshadowed by his contemporary Django Reinhardt, the gypsy guitarist from Belgium.

Both Bunn and Reinhardt used strong melodic lines and both played acoustic steel-string guitars, Bunn on a Gibson Super 400 arch-top and Reinhardt on a French-made flat-top cutaway designed by Mario Maccaferri. Both had different conceptions of sound in mind – Teddy Bunn played using the thumb of his right hand while Django used a hard pick.

It's fruitless to guess what the results might have been had Django not been somewhat incapacitated by his left-hand limitations. They both played by ear, rather than from formal music notation, and neither played from chord symbols, yet they both produced a quite different guitar sound, each drawing on his own environmental background. It's for these reasons that I bracket the two players together, so as to illustrate historically how two equally inventive, natural jazz executants can be contrasting and equally attractive and yet divergent from the mainstream.

Django's background is very well known, but Teddy Bunn's background isn't as well chronicled. It may therefore interest the reader to know that I became acquainted with both musicians' playing style at almost a parallel period (between 1933 and 1938). However, although I met Django on a few occasions when he came to London in 1938, I never actually met Teddy Bunn.

One person who did, however, was Peter Tanner, and his story of Bunn in the 6 February 1943 edition of *Melody Maker* begins, 'It is a curious thing that, although Teddy Bunn has been playing and recording for a very long time, it wasn't until 1938 that his work became at all well known, both over here and in the States. In fact, in 1939, when I asked Teddy Bunn to give me some facts concerning himself,

he expressed astonishment that he should have been heard of at all in England. "Man, you're just foolin' me," he said, and was only partially convinced when I showed him Ivor Mairants' article "Taking The Bunn", which had appeared in the *Melody Maker* some months previously... I had great difficulty in persuading him to play any of his own recordings; he much preferred those of Eddie Lang and Segovia, his two favourite guitar players, with Lonnie Johnson coming up close behind.'

In another *Melody Maker* article, this time from the '40s, there's a review of six mid-month swing record issues, which reads as follows: 'Willie [the Lion] Smith enters into two, while O'Neil Spencer plays and swings on three and Teddy Bunn is also on the above three. If you read Ivor Mairants' excellent analysis of Brother Bunn, you will find him in a total of 40 solo bars on the [Milt] Herth record, which is otherwise the weakest of the three discs, "Home Cooking With The Frying Pan"/"La De Daddy Doo" (Brunswick 02691).'

Apart from being a member of The Spirits Of Rhythm for five years when they played at the Onyx Club on 52nd Street, New York, Teddy Bunn recorded with a number of other combinations, and the following list of representative recordings (British releases) will furnish as much information about his activities as any other description: 'The Washboards Get Together' (HMV B6114), with The Washboard Serenaders; 'I Got Rhythm' (BRUNS 01715) and 'I've Got The World On A String', with The Spirits Of Rhythm; 'Beale Street Mama', with The Bob Howard Orchestra (VOC S233); 'Melancholy' (VOC S207); 'Bump It' (VOC S209) and 'Four Or Five Times' (VOC 209), with Johnny Dodds' Orchestra; 'Tired Of Fattening Frogs' (VOC S274), with Rosetta Crawford And Orchestra; 'Ja Da' (HMV B9236), with The Tommy Ladnier Orchestra; and 'Just Another Woman' (HMV B9261), with The Hot Lips Page Trio. USA releases include 'If You See Me Coming' (Bluebird B100087), with The Mezzrow-Ladnier Quintet; 'Money Is Honey' (US Decca 2470), with The Ramblers; 'Rockin' The Blues' (Blue Note 3), with The Port Of Harlem Jazzmen; 'Summertime' (Blue

Note 6), with The Sidney Bechet Quintet; 'Guitar On High'/'Bachelor Blue' (Blue Note 503/504); 'It's Sweet Like So' (Victor 38592), with Spencer Williams; and 'Evil Man Blues' (Bluebird 8364), with The Hot Lips Page Trio. (This list appeared in *Melody Maker* on 7 February 1954 and is used by kind permission.)

'Four Or Five Times' has always been a favourite Bunn solo of mine, in which he swings all the time, right from a low-pitched first phrase. In the fourth bar, the F-to-G♭ bends lead into ascending triplets, rounded off by a bar of C♭s in a heavy blues style.

Charlie Christian must have heard this record, because he certainly embraced these runs, not to mention the clever variation of triplets in bar ten. Bars 13–19 consist of a terrific build-up of excitement before continuing in four completely contrasting bars of fourths, while the last twelve bars are worthy of a place in the greatest of jazz compositions. I'm sure that there were a number of takes before this master was chosen.

I hope that, after this chapter, Teddy Bunn will no longer be a stranger to guitarists. He is certainly the connecting link between Lang and Christian.

I've Got The World On A String (Arlen and Koehler)

Recorded 20 November 1933, New York. ARC Test Recording (XTO 1336-1) and Brunswick 01997. Recorded by The Spirits Of Rhythm: Leo Watson, Douglas Daniels (vocals), Teddy Bunn (guitar) and Virgil Scroggins (drums, vocals).

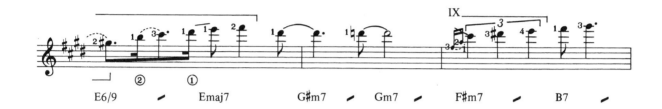

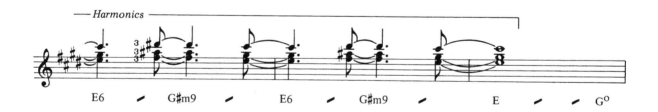

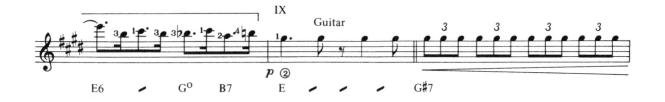

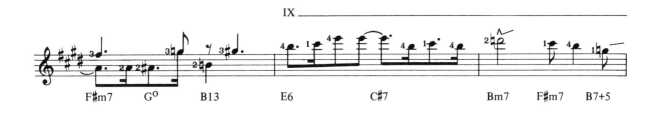

Way Down Yonder In New Orleans (Creamer and Layton)

Recorded 1936 and released on Brunswick 01997A (38633). Teddy Bunn with Red McKenzie and The Spirits Of Rhythm.

Four Or Five Times (Byron)

Recorded 1938 and released on Vocalion S209B (628331). Teddy Bunn with Jimmy Noone and his orchestra. Vocal chorus by O'Neil Spencer.

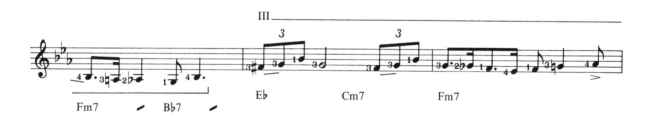

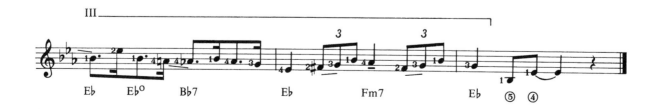

9 DJANGO REINHARDT

'Dinah' (Akst, Lewis and Young)
'Chasing Shadows' (Silver and Davis)
'Ain't Misbehavin'' (Brooks, Razaf and Waller)
'Nuages' (Reinhardt and Larne)

Now for the guitarist who strayed most from the mainstream. Unlike Teddy Bunn, who isn't as well known, even among musicians, the popularity of Django Reinhardt (born Jean Baptiste Reinhardt, 23 January 1910, Liverchies, Belgium, died 16 May 1953, Fontainebleau, France) has grown and grown. In fact, during the years since 1953, when Django suffered a fatal heart attack, his popularity has risen beyond all normal expectations, embracing a wider field of players and new generations, from classical players to young rock guitarists from Les Paul to Joe Pass. Les Paul admired Django so much that, on hearing that there hadn't been a decent tombstone placed on Django's grave, he insisted on providing one, even going to the lengths of periodically sending an emissary to place some flowers on the grave, instructing him to report back on the condition of the stone.

The music that Django played in his lifetime is so appreciated that – dare I say it? – it has signs of becoming immortal. Although he never played the jazz of the Lang/Johnson/Bunn/Christian school, his improvisations have infiltrated the jazz of generations of international guitarists – American, British, European and Far Eastern – and that is the greatest tribute that can be bestowed on a player who is no longer with us in the flesh.

Django made his recording debut in a Paris studio in 1933, when he was aged 23, accompanied by a group comprising two guitars and bass directed by jazz violinist Stephane Grappelli, a group that became known as Le Quintet Du Hot Club De France. From the outset, my personal interest was directed more toward Django than to Grappelli, who was billed as the leader, because I considered Django the greater inventive and innovative genius of the two. Nevertheless, I tried to base my personal style on the American jazz wizards that I've so far mentioned. It would be dishonest of me to state otherwise, even considering the hindsight of more than half a century.

Quoting from my autobiography, *My 50 Fretting Years*, 'The Quintet first received public acclaim in England in 1935, when their records were first issued on the Oriole label. It was not until January 1938 that the Quintet came to London and a small group of guitarists, including myself, went around to [Django's] hotel [the Regent Palace] to give him a warm welcome.

'[The Quintet] opened at the Cambridge Theatre in London. This was a Sunday concert and in an intimate, comfortable, newly built auditorium facing an audience of musicians and fans. Excitement ran high. It resulted in what must have been the most thrilling audience appreciation of their tour, because the dates that followed were commercial bookings at suburban variety theatres. They played at the Shepherds Bush and Wood Green Empires to sparsely filled halls...

'Whenever I could, I sat in the dressing room between shows watching Django wield his hard pick on his Maccaferri guitar. He used downstrokes, except in tremolo passages, and hit the strings very near the bridge, not resting his fingers but working from the wrist and elbow.

'As most people know, the third and fourth fingers of Django's left hand were permanently bent from the middle knuckle, a disability caused by a fire. Nevertheless, he was able to finger a variety of interesting chords when aided by the use of his strong index and middle fingers. The stretch between his first and second fingers easily encompassed three frets, so that he could play diminished runs, ie...

...using fingers one and two and shifting up a fret when ascending (except between the third and second strings) and reversing the fingering – 2, 1, 2, 1 – on the way down.

'His music fascinated me – he never played a wrong note – but his gypsy style did not draw me sufficiently to desire to imitate his improvisations in the way, say, Teddy Bunn's solos did...

'His tour with Duke Ellington in the US is often spoken about by guitarists but is generally considered to have been a disappointment to all concerned, except for the few guitarists that gathered at the home of Harry Volpe...'

Harry Volpe was then a leading New York guitarist who had become a friend and guide to Django during his stay in the US. He related to me that he had invited Django to his home after the first show, hoping that he would play, but Django refused to be drawn. However, the second night was different: 'I had invited a few guitarists around to meet him and he performed musical miracles late into the night. He was absolutely wonderful and I will never forget it.'

After his US visit, he acquired a pick-up, but I don't think that he sounds the same Django as he doesn when playing his acoustic guitar. One has but to listen to *Album Of Djangology* (Vogue, 1974) to hear the difference between the warmth of the individual, personal sound of his acoustic guitar and the more impassive, urbane tones of his electric-guitar playing.

What, then, has been the basis of Django's overriding talent? In my opinion, there are several facets: timing, vibrato, attack, intensity of expression and conviction, strongly felt and unhesitatingly delivered. These factors forged the arrowhead that pierced the ear and heart of the listener.

According to personal opinions voiced by leading jazz guitarists today, he has become one of the three main influences (the other two being Charlie Christian and Wes Montgomery), and he has, of course, influenced players whose styles are quite different from one another's, such as Les Paul, Barney Kessel, Chet Atkins and Joe Pass, to name but a few.

Each player influenced by Django must have favourite renderings by which they are most inspired. I, too, have favourites, but have limited my choice here to four, which was extremely difficult. However, among other considerations, I selected solos recorded at different periods and played at different tempi, in varying tone colours and – in the case of 'Nuages' (of which he recorded many versions) – with a different combination of players. Even so, there must be performances in his repertoire with which I am unfamiliar.

The first of the four is 'Dinah', the first title to be recorded by Le Quintet Du Hot Club De France. Django was to live another 20 years after this recording, during which time he was to provide posterity with a vast output of recordings, making his playing instantly recognisable and his name universally known, but his rating just four years after that first recording session (during which he also played 'Lady Be Good', 'I Saw Stars', 'Tiger Rag' and 'Dark

Eyes') is revealed by the first *Melody Maker* jazz poll, run in 1937, in which the results were as follows: International section (guitar) – first, Eddie Lang (1,737 votes, the highest cast for any section, even though Eddie had died in 1933); second, Django Reinhardt (245 votes); third, Dick McDonough (83 votes); fourth, Albert Harris (54 votes); fifth, Allan Reuss (45 votes); sixth, George Van Eps (28 votes); seventh, Eddie Condon (22 votes); eighth, Carl Kress and Leonard Lucie (16 votes). British section (guitar) – first, Albert Harris (1,287 votes); second, Ivor Mairants (on tour with Roy Fox, 438 votes); third, Danny Perri (36 votes).

My second choice, 'Chasing Shadows', is a complete contrast to 'Dinah', displaying Django's warmest feelings on the lower strings of the guitar, while the third, 'Ain't Misbehavin'', is much happier, and the fourth, 'Nuages', is of course his own composition. As I've already mentioned, there are a number of recordings of 'Nuages', but this is my favourite, recorded in 1947 and played at a comfortable tempo.

I don't intend to go into deep analysis of the four solos but rather to briefly note the most salient points. One may observe the contrast between the rather simplistic beginning of 'Dinah' and the lyrical lead-in to 'Nuages'. One cannot fail to be charmed by the free, unspoiled freshness of the first chorus of 'Dinah', which ends in a high trill leading into a non-stop descending group of semitone triplets. The middle-eight, played in octaves in a somewhat plaintive mode, became one of Django's tools many years before Wes Montgomery appeared on the scene. The solo is brought to an end with a somewhat gypsy, repetitive four bars of triplets before closing on a positive chordal note.

In 'Chasing Shadows', Django caresses the melody in fat-sounding, rounded lower notes on the lower strings, which he bends in true jazz fashion before ending the first 16 bars in a flurry, leading to a middle- and higher-register middle-eight. In contrast, the last eight bars wind down into the lower register before ending in true blues fashion higher up the register again. It's still one of my favourites.

'Ain't Misbehavin'' offers a typical, middle-of-the-road, bouncy performance, even though this is slightly flawed by a couple of doubtful notes in the tenth and eleventh bars, in which, harmonically, Django dives in and out of a little melodic clash.

As for 'Nuages', I've mentioned the delicious lead-in after the initial clarinet solo, which states the melody, and, since that figure has already been stated, Django delves right in with an improvised chorus. The clarinet then re-enters and, together with the guitar, plays a rhythmic *tutti* four bars before the clarinet takes up the next three bars and a beat, with Django providing a characteristic chord tremolo accompaniment. Then comes his lead-in to the next four bars (which the Italians would term '*delicioso*') before the clarinet takes us out with the melody, accompanied by guitar arpeggios, and so to the final arpeggiated chords. The whole solo, in fact, makes a memorable and fitting finale to the genius of Django.

Dinah (Akst, Lewis and Young)

Recorded December 1934. Released on Oriole String Style series LV100 (P27161). Reissued on Vogue VJD 502/1 Jazz Double. Django Reinhardt and Le Quintet Du Hot Club De France: Stephane Grappelli (violin), Django Reinhardt (solo guitar), Roger Chaput, Joseph Reinhardt (guitars) and Louis Vola (bass).

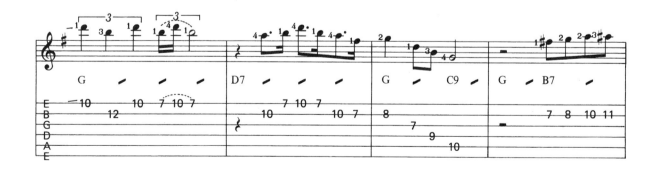

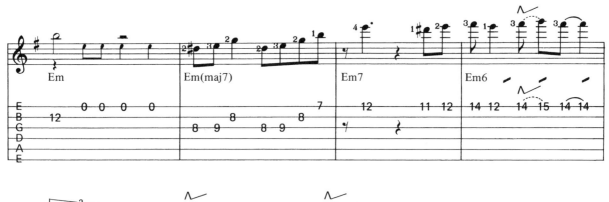

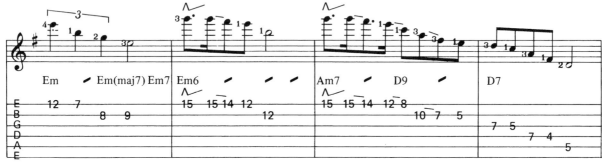

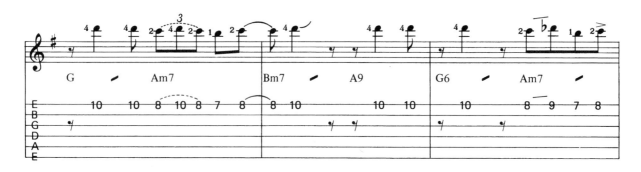

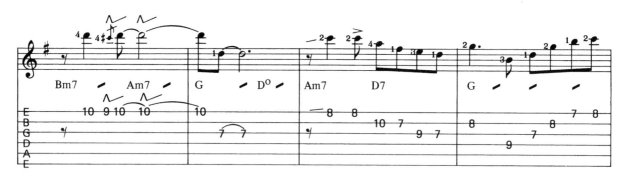

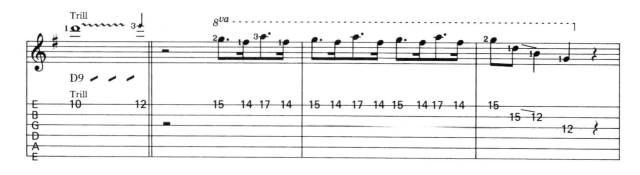

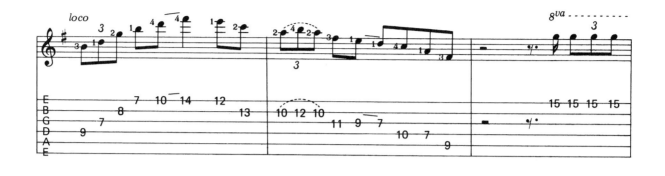

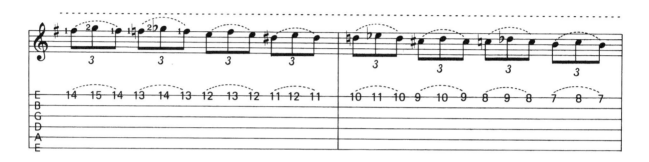

Chasing Shadows (Silver and Davis)

Released on Decca F6002/77531. Stephane Grappelli and his Hot Four, featuring Django Reinhardt (guitar).

Ain't Misbehavin' (Waller, Brooks and Razaf)

Recorded 22 April 1937 and released on OLA 1708-1, HMV B8690. Le Quintet Du Hot Club De France: Django Reinhardt (guitar), Stephane Grappelli (violin), Louis Vola (bass), Pierre Ferret and Marcel Bianchi (guitars).

Eb / Cm7   Fm7 / Bb9   Eb / G7+   Ab / Abm D°   Eb6 / Gb13 /

Fm7 / Bb7   Eb Cm6 Fm7 /   Bb11 /   Bb7

With abandon and long slurs

Eb Cm7   Fm7 / Bb9 /   Eb / G7+ /   Ab Abm

Eb   Gb7   Fm7   Bb7   Eb / C7

C7   F7 Bb7 /   Eb / Cm7   Fm / Bb9 /

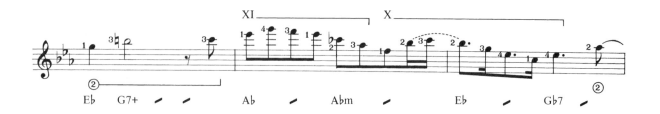

Eb G7+ / /   Ab / Abm /   Eb / Gb7 /

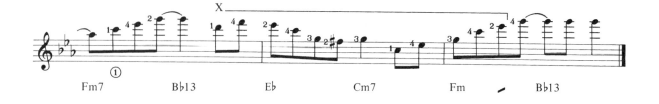

Fm7   Bb13   Eb   Cm7   Fm / Bb13

Nuages (Reinhardt)

Recorded 25 August 1947, Paris. Reissued on Jazz Vogue (Pye Records VSD 5021). Django Reinhardt (solo guitar), Maurice Mounier (clarinet), Eddie Bernard (piano), Eugene Vees (guitar), Emanuel Soudieux (bass) and Macques Martinon (drums).

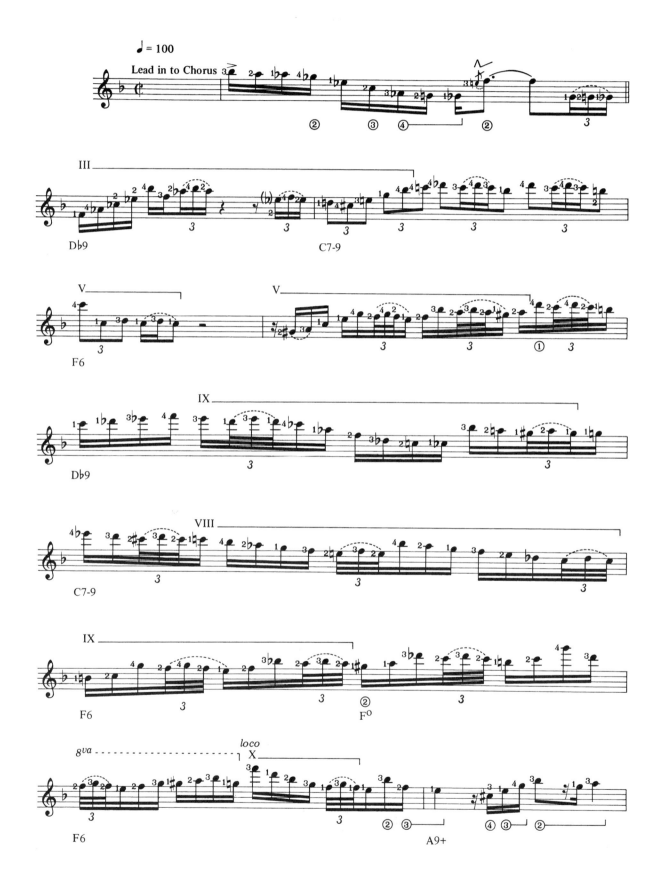

© 1941 Publications Francis Day SA. Peter Maurice Music Co Ltd, London WC2H 0QY (50%). Reproduced by permission of IMP Ltd.

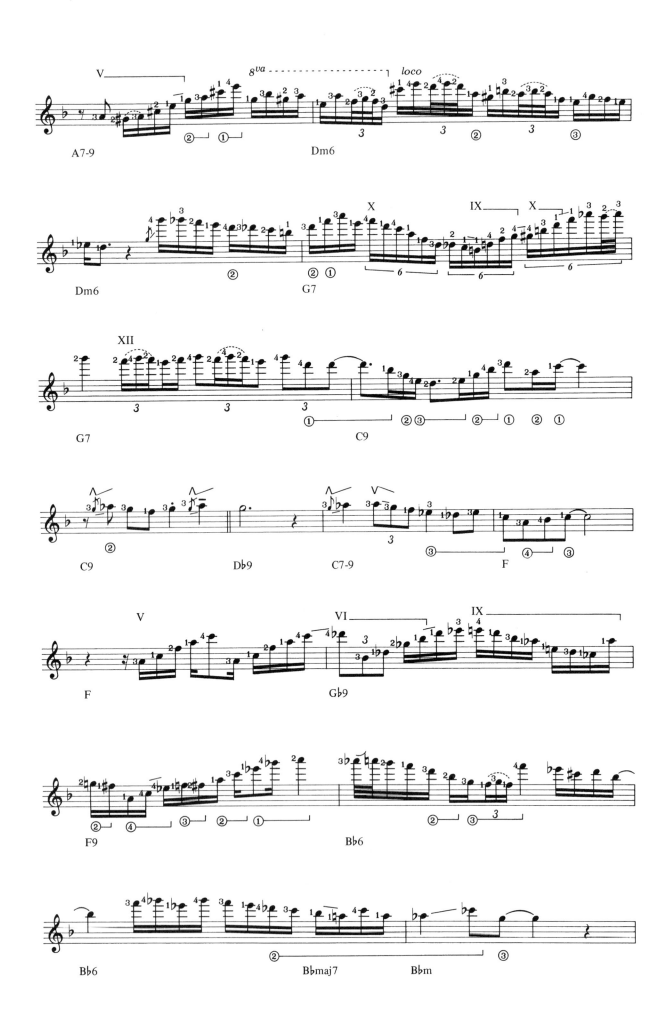

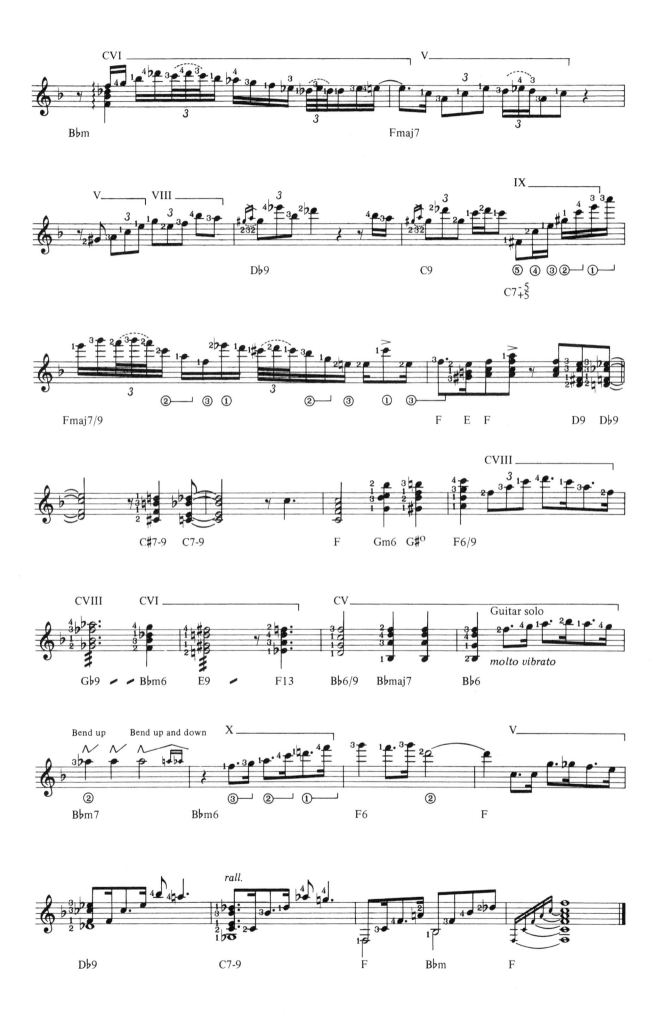

10 OSCAR ALEMAN

'Whispering' (Shonberger, Rose and Coburn)

Oscar Marcelo Aleman was born in Argentina between 1905 and 1910, according to different sources, and died in Buenos Aires in 1980. After working theere initially, he went to Europe, formed a duo known as Los Lobos and worked in Spain. The duo then split up and Aleman then went to Paris, where in 1933 he joined American expatriate Freddy Taylor's band on guitar.

His guitar was the National all-metal, six-string, three-resonator model, and it was with this instrument that he gained fame in Paris. He later joined the band that accompanied Joséphine Baker, recorded with clarinettist Danny Polo and led a band at the Chantilly Club in Paris. His sojourn in Paris lasted until 1941, when he returned to Buenos Aires to resume playing and teaching.

Had his fame not diminished over the ensuing years, he might have been a controversial figure in the field of jazz guitar, since some critics stated, that his jazz 'bowed in the Reinhardt direction while still remaining close to Teddy Bunn's concept'. However, Aleman had all but forgotten him, and accordingly, in his solo of 'Whispering' (part of which I've transcribed here), he didn't really offer a new direction in jazz or any other field, for that matter, while at the same time his contemporaries Reinhardt and Bunn have influenced guitarists ever since their work was first heard.

It must be admitted that Aleman played rhythmically and with confidence but that the jazz content of his music was very muddled. In this recorded solo of 'Whispering', the Palm Court introduction leads into a single-line melody with the type of arpeggio accompaniment more in keeping with an early-19th-century guitar *étude*. Then, after a two-bar rhythmic chordal introduction, the second chorus begins in a style reminiscent of the banjo, with the chordal melody shifting up and down in semitones until the seventh and eighth bars, where the chords change to rhythmic arpeggios.

Bars eleven and twelve consist of F7 chords on the inside four strings, played so that the E♭ (or D♯) on the second string clashes with open E (first string), thereby creating a blues effect. This would have been a good trick, if the ensuing bars could have followed in a logical way.

Unfortunately, the other effects are unrelated. From the 14th bar, the style changes again to single notes, with an odd rhythm in bars 15 and 16, almost falling to pieces before the single-note melody is somewhat restored, leading to a diminished run and then an A arpeggio. From bars 21–22, the chordal, shifting melody is again evident until bars 27 and 28, employing harmonics in what sounds like a circus acrobat jumping though a hoop. The phrasing then settles down for two bars and even includes a blue note.

Bar 31 contains a triplet quotation from the first piece in Grieg's *Peer Gynt Suite No 1*, 'Morning Mood', leading into bar 32, which consists of a jazz phrase. This is followed by the first two bars of a modulation into another jazz chorus that is even more weird and wonderful.

Oscar Aleman fits into this slot well because of his National guitar (as played by Eddie Durham) and his close proximity in Paris to Django, but that's about the closest his playing resembled that of either.

Whispering (Shonberger, Rose and Coburn)

Recorded 5 December 1938, Paris. Released on Pathé (F), Oscar Aleman TMO CO54. Aleman played a National Resophonic all-metal guitar.

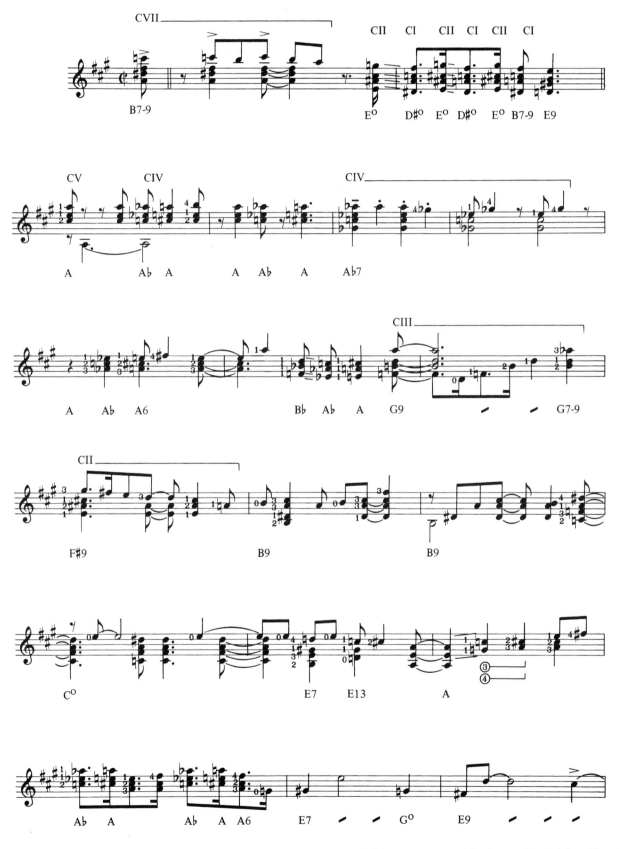

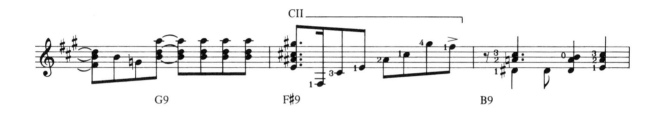

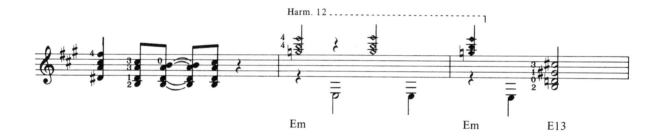

11 EDDIE DURHAM

'Hittin' The Bottle' (Arlen and Koehler)
'Love Me Or Leave Me' (Donaldson and Kahn)

Eddie Durham (born 29 August 1906, San Marcos, Texas, died 6 March 1987, New York) was reputed to be the first guitarist to have amplified his instrument. He is also credited as having introduced the amplified guitar to Charlie Christian, and for that jazz guitarists are truly thankful.

As previously noted, the jazz guitar developed in the years between 1927 and 1937, very much through the influences of guitarists Lang, Johnson, McDonough, Van Eps, Reuss, Bunn and Reinhardt. An influence not generally perceived until well after 1937, however, is the guitar playing of Eddie Durham. Although featured with Jimmy Lunceford's orchestra, and also a member of Basie's and Calloway's bands, The Kansas City Six and other small groups, Durham's influence wasn't general in nature but was mainly limited to black players. But if his influence was limited, it was through his early experiments with amplification that the guitar moved to achieve greater popularity.

His arranging ability and his trombone playing in various bands probably diffused his importance as a jazz-guitar soloist, but when he introduced the electric guitar to Charlie Christian in 1937 he caused the fundamental change that brought Christian to the attention of Benny Goodman, and the rest is history.

Musically, one can detect the influence of Eddie Durham in Charlie Chrisitan's distribution of across-the-fingerboard runs. Notice the 13ths, ninths and the placing of blue notes in Durham's playing, which must surely have influenced Christian.

Thus Eddie Durham seems to be the guitarist best fitted to bridge the acoustic and amplified eras in this unfolding of jazz-guitar history.

Hittin' The Bottle (Arlen and Koehler)

Recorded 30 September 1935. Released on Brunswick 02133B (MX60016A). Eddie Durham with The Jimmy Lunceford Orchestra.

then you sleep a-round a bit be care-ful not to hit that bot-tle___ Woah

just like a clown start mess-in' a-round___ keep

go-in' to town then you make a break then you wig-gle like a snake that's

hit-tin' that bot-tle___ it's ea - sy to do___ cause

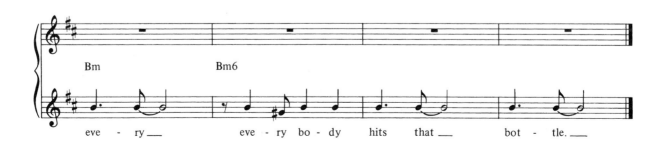

eve - ry___ eve - ry bo - dy hits that ___ bot - tle. ___

Love Me Or Leave Me (Donaldson and Kahn)

Recorded 18 March 1938, New York. Released on Commodore (MX22583). Eddie Durham and Freddie Greene (rhythm guitar) with Buck Clayton (trumpet), Walter Page (string bass) and Joe Jones (drums).

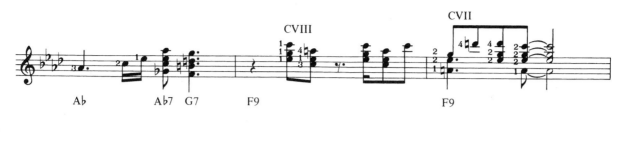

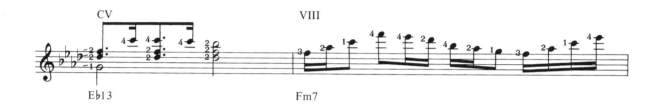

12 CHARLIE CHRISTIAN

'I Surrender, Dear' (Barris and Clifford)
'The Sheik Of Araby' (Smith, Wheeler and Snyder)
'Honeysuckle Rose' (Waller and Razaf)

Charlie Christian was born in Dallas, Texas, on 29 July 1916 and died on 2 March 1942 in Staten Island Hospital, New York. Although his life story has often been repeated by writers on the subject, there are still guitarists to whom the name is unfamiliar. It would therefore be remiss of me to ignore the younger strata.

Charlie Christian was brought up in Oklahoma City and, due to the fact that his father was a guitarist and therefore an influence on Charlie's musical upbringing, he was working in his first professional job by the time he was 15. There is also evidence to suggest that he was influenced by a personal meeting with Eddie Durham, who was reputed to be the original jazz performer on the electric guitar.

In as early as 1937, Charlie Christian had added a pick-up to his guitar and attached it to an amplifier. Therefore, when the famous jazz pianist Mary Lou Williams heard him play while she was on tour, she was immediately attracted and raved about him to her influential friend, the wealthy businessman and impresario John Hammond.

Hammond heard Christian play and was determined to place him with Benny Goodman's band, which was then playing at the Victor Hugo Club in Beverly Hills, California. Goodman agreed to hear Christian, and according to an interview with John Hammond published in *Down Beat* on 25 August 1966, Christian arrived in Los Angeles in August 1939 and was later that night 'smuggled' onto the bandstand. The band began the session with 'Rose Room' and after they played the opening chorus Goodman pointed to Charlie to take a chorus. This chorus, it was reported, stretched to 45 minutes!

Goodman engaged Christian on the spot and, after some sartorial remoulding, the guitarist took his place as a permanent member of the band, which at the time included Lionel Hampton on vibraphone. The band returned from Beverly Hills to New York in late 1939 and, in one of their first recording sessions, made history with 'Rose Room' and 'Flying Home', both issued on the disc.

Although the credits named Christian, Goodman and Hampton as composers, I've always been of the opinion that 'Flying Home' was a pure Charlie Christian guitar phrase, embellished by The Goodman Septet. Fifty years or so later, I listened to a BBC jazz programme broadcast on 21 November 1992 that included an interview with the famous tenor-sax player and bandleader, and to my pleasure the presenter said that Charlie Christian was the greatest jazz musician of his time. He then recalled the many visits he'd paid to Minton's Harlem Jazz Club, where Christian often jammed, and the wonderful original improvisations that Christian produced, which were promptly garnered by the many famous jazz musicians present, who had also come to Minton's to listen to Christian and harvest the rich jazz pasture and use it as their own.

Without doubt, 'Flying Home' was the fruit of Christian's original mind. The tune (coupled with 'Rose Room') was published in England on Parlophone R2917/WO026133 and guitar history was made. The electric guitar had broken the sound barrier.

With a salary of $2,000 per week, instead of the $10 a week he earned in far-off Oklahoma, Charlie, who was always prone to TB, disregarded his health and lived a high old life with girls on the one hand and late nights at Minton's Harlem Jazz Club on the other.

Other famous jazz musicians (apart from resident pianist Thelonious Monk) were regular visitors, and the music of Dizzy Gillespie and Charlie Parker – the originators of bebop, among others – wasn't lost on Christian, who spread the word on guitar style, followed by the greats of the '40s.

The electric guitar was here to stay, and so was the style that affected the next two generations of jazz guitarists, until Wes Montgomery shifted the goalposts. Unfortunately, because of his deteriorating health, Charlie wasn't given more than three creative years for further development. He was hospitalised in June 1941 and died on 2 March 1942.

As many guitarists are aware, Charlie's output with The Goodman Band and Septet was very generous. There is also another important source from which one can add to his output. For these recordings of Charlie's uninhibited improvisations we owe a debt to Jerry Newman, a jazz fan and recording expert. From time to time, he would take his recording equipment along to Minter's and record Christian's playing onto acetates. These discs were discovered five years after Charlie had died and were published on the Vox label on one album. If this record is still available, get it.

'Rose Room', released on the Parlophone disc *Super Swing Music* No.49 R2917 (WOO 26133), commences with a four-bar introduction in harmony played by clarinet, guitar and vibes. The piece is in the key of A♭ yet beings not on the tonic chord but on the dominant chord of E♭13 and continues for 16 bars before repeating (ie not AABA for four bars each but A for 16 bars, repeated with a variation).

The solo improvisation stays in the sixth position for six beats before making a characteristic downward slur to the fourth position, enabling the chord to be substituted to E♭11–9 using the A♭, the fourth (or eleventh) of the chord, and slipping in the minor ninth (E♮), leading naturally to the tonic A♭ chord for two bars before turning into a chord of A♭7. Bars six and seven then lead onto D7, the final chord of the first eight-bar phrase.

There is then a characteristic gap between a lead-in of four quavers and, for the third time in the first eight bars, another two-fret descending slur down to the first position, where the chord changes from D♭ to D♭m. Then, in bar ten of the chorus, the minor third of D♭ (E or F♭) is strongly emphasised by being sustained for a whole bar before changing to F13, leading to B♭9 in bar 13, a long rest in bar 14 and an exciting turnaround in bars 15 and 16, leading right into the second half of the chorus again on the chord of E♭13.

In bars 17 and 18, instead of sticking rigidly to the notes of E♭13 (ie E♭, G, B♭, D♭, F, C and A♭), the fourth is again employed descending to G, then D♮ is used as a suspension to D♭. By using A♭ in the second half of bar 18, the chord changes to B♭m7, which leads to A♭.

There now follows a new idea, where the tenth and ninth of the chord are used as a pivot followed by a near-triplet, and this idea goes on for four bars, while the last eight consist of a build-up to the finish and draw on another Christian trick: the augmented fourth, or tritone, between the F and B.

In bars 27 and 28, where one would normally use

| A♭ / G♭ / | F7 / / / |

Christian instead uses

| A♭ / / / | B♭m6 / F7 B♭ / | Fm7 / B♭7/1 |
27　　　　　　28　　　　　　29

　　　E♭9 / / / | A♭ / / / | A♭ / / / |
　　　　30　　　　31　　　　32

Bar 30 is enhanced by various blue notes (ie B♮ and G♭ in an E♭9 chord to lead to the tonic, A♭).

Christian can be both contemplative and exciting when he goes into overdrive, for instance in the double-tempo passage in the third and fourth bars of 'I Surrender, Dear', the first of Christian's pieces transcribed here. If the listener wonders why Christian's improvisations sound as they do, a study of the overall shapes of the phrases and the placing of the notation will provide some clues.

One can be subjective and say how deliciously attractive the piece sounds or objective and study the placement of the notes. For instance, bar one begins with the third of the chord, F, and descends by way of D (the tonic) to A (the fifth of D minor). The following bar continues on the descent by commencing on the seventh of the next chord and ascending through the third (C♯), the fifth (E) and the octave (G) of the starting note, completely omitting the root, A.

In the E7 chord in bar three, the starting note is the major third, G♯. It continues with the fifth, seventh and ninth, again reaching the apex with the 13th (C♯). Similarly, the same treatment is meted out to the D13 chord in the second half of bar four.

This short solo is well worth studying for its phrasing, its notation and because playing it is a pleasure. It is likewise because of the uniquely Christian phrasing that I couldn't bring myself to omit the next Christian piece, 'The Sheik Of Araby', which is followed by 'Honeysuckle Rose'.

In 'The Sheik Of Araby', Christian waits for the ensemble chord of B♭ to begin the first bar before entering after three quavers in order to make a short, two-bar statement. This pattern is repeated in the third bar, although in bar four there is a rest of half a bar before the four-quaver run leads into a strong, flowing, long sentence, which comes to a halt in bar eleven. Bar 16 reflects bar one and leads into the second half.

In fact, every solo uses a different device as a jumping-off point. In 'Honeysuckle Rose', the guitar leads into the solo before the first full-melody bar and so figuratively starts off on a different foot.

From the very lead-in, the across-the-board, arpeggiated 13th chord, with the emphasis on the 13th (F), pronounce the Charlie Christian style. This short, two-bar statement is followed by a diatonic run commencing on the fifth of the seventh chord, A♭, and descending to the root of the chord in bar four before eventually leading to the tonic (D♭) in bar five, right on to bar eight.

In bar six, however, the tonic descends onto a blue note (C♭) and ascends through a leading passing note (E♮) to a strong major arpeggio of the tonic (D♭) but leaves a breathing space on the first beat of bar eight. This quaver rest permits a clear lead-in to the second phrase. It then flows uninterrupted to bar twelve, where it comes to a natural halt, but not before engaging some interesting suspensions (ie A♮-A♭-G♮ in bar nine).

In bar eleven, an innocent descending run of E♭, D♭, C and B♭ doesn't fall on A♭, as would be expected, but on A♮ (the minor ninth of the chord A♭7) before coming to rest on A♭ in the twelfth bar. Incidentally, in bar eleven, Christian makes use of an inverted tritone (A♮ to E♭), playing instead E♭ to A♮. The tritone was one of Christian's favourite intervals.

Bar 17 again makes use of the across-the-board arpeggiated 13th chord, but this time it's D♭13 instead of the A♭13 found at the beginning. The first string bend comes in bar 23, on F (the 13th of the chord), and then descends diatonically and ascends as an arpeggio to finish the run on the 24th bar.

The last eight bars commence with a four-in-a-bar drive, building up to the 28th bar, where the diatonic run from E♭ down the scale again lands on A♮, as in bar eleven, but then continues to A♭, leading on the end, but not before a pronounced bend from E♭ to E in the penultimate bar.

In my opinion, the tightness of the orchestral arrangement coming in on the last bar of the solo rather cramps the build-up of the guitar ending.

I Surrender, Dear (Barris and Clifford)

Released on Parlophone Super Rhythm series 116, R2757 (WOO26743). Charlie Christian with The Benny Goodman Sextet.

The Sheik Of Araby (Smith, Wheeler and Snyder)

Recorded 1940 and released on Parlophone Super Rhythm series 110, R2753 (WOO26718). Charlie Christian with The Benny Goodman Sextet.

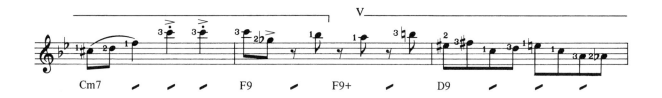

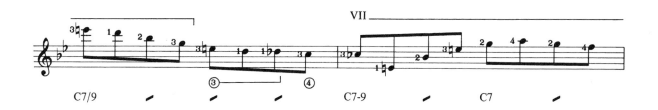

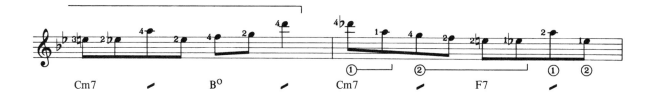

Honeysuckle Rose (Waller and Razaf)

Released on Columbia WCD26290 DB5010, Super Swing Music series number 159. Charlie Christian with The Benny Goodman Orchestra.

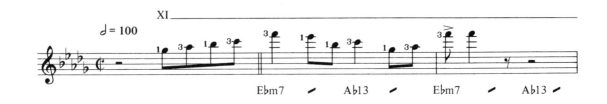

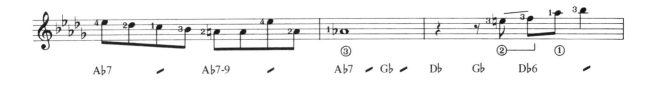

PART 2

THE BEBOP ERA

INTRODUCTION

Bebop began in 1913 but, as Dizzy Gillespie once said, 'No one man or group of men started modern jazz.' Dizzy's friend and contemporary Charlie Parker had at the time been getting bored with the stereotyped chord changes used by jazz musicians and, while practising 'Cherokee', discovered that, by piling up additional intervals to the basic harmonies and then using those extended harmonies as a basis for improvisation of the original melodic lines, supported by the appropriately related chord changes, he could develop the lines and breathe new life into those melodies.

It's therefore no wonder that jazz musicians – both executants and writers – who were familiar with some of the work of serious (ie classical) composers cite JS Bach and Claude Debussy among their favourite composers, Bach for his form, fugue and counterpoint and Debussy for his use of compound harmonies, such as ninths, elevenths and whole-tone chords. In fact, when Charlie Parker spoke to me in Paris at the 1949 European Jazz Festival, in which he was taking part, he mentioned his admiration for Debussy's music and was neither alone nor the first in doing so.

Composer/conductor Constant Lambert (born 1905, died 1951) discusses these resonances and their bearing on music in a succinct way in his book *Music Ho*, stating, 'There are few harmonic combinations in early Debussy that cannot be found in Liszt... The difference in their use is, however, that while Liszt employed these combinations of chords as a point of stress in a continuous line of thought...Debussy draws our attention to this harmony as an entity in itself, with its own powers of evocation.' He goes on to illustrate, 'When one reads a sentence using a particular word within the sentence, one might not make a point of analysing it, as with an Egyptian hieroglyphic or a Chinese ideogram.'

In quite a different way, and in very different circumstances, Parker, Gillespie, Thelonious Monk and others who used to jam at Minton's Club in New York would work out complex variations on the regular chords during rehearsals and develop them during performances.

Bebop continued to develop during the '40s, when the boppers used more complex chords with higher extension and altered notes, such as flattened and augmented fifths, etc, and in so doing made available a greater selection of pitches and a freer use of passing notes.

The boppers – Charlie Parker, Dizzy Gillespie, Thelonious Monk, Tadd Dameron and others – then began to write tunes based on these extended harmonies, including the blues, and also reharmonised and altered the melodies of the standards – 'What Is This Thing Called Love' became 'Hothouse', 'How High The Moon' became 'Ornithology', 'I Got Rhythm' became 'Anthropology', and so on. Although bebop was considered to be rather a cult music in the '40s and didn't achieve great popularity, it laid the foundations for its development in the '50s and '60s. There are some basic features in bebop, such as adding thirds to existing major, minor and dominant seventh chords, as overleaf. For further examples, transpose the above to all keys.

G B D F♯ A C♯ E = Gmaj7/9♯11/13, extending the range
from the key of G to A, ie dual tonality

G B♭ D F♯ A C♯ E = Gm maj7/9♯11/13

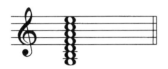

G B D F A C E = G13

G B D F A♭ C E = G13–9

G B D♭ F A♭ (C) E = G13–5–9

13 CARMEN MASTREN

'Two Moods' (Mastren)

It is with particular affection that I write about my old friend Carmen Mastren, who was the closest of my American guitar buddies. Even before we ever met, his career seemed to be similar to my own. In New York, he was a popular sessioner and a member of various leading dance bands, including of course Tommy Dorsey's band. He played an Epiphone Emperor guitar similar to my own and he also wrote guitar solos, including 'Two Moods', but in one respect he had an advantage: he was an excellent orchestrator, scoring for Dorsey arrangements of the widely known 'Song Of India' and 'Black Eyes'. Among his colleagues were the famous drummer Buddy Rich and the even more famous Frank Sinatra, and at times it was Carmen's patience and bonhomie that separated the two famous artists from getting at each other.

Carmen Nicholas Mastandrea Cohses (born 6 October 1913, died 31 March 1981) was born in New York to a musical family (his older brother, Al, was a fine trombonist), and in 1937 he was sufficiently well known among jazz fans and players to win top placing in the *Down Beat* readers' poll. I first heard him play on a recording of 'Farewell Biues' and 'Swinging At The Famous Door' (a club on 52nd Street, New York) with The Delta Four that I thought was the epitome of rhythm-guitar playing. The other musicians on that recording were Joe Marsala (clarinet), Roy Eldridge (trumpet) and Sid Weiss (bass).

Carmen went on to join Tommy Dorsey's band and was with him for a number of years, until Captain Glenn Miller plucked him out early in 1943 to become a member of one of the finest rhythm sections ever assembled. The other members of The American Air Force Band's rhythm section were Trigger Alpert (bass), Mel Powell (piano) and Ray McKinley (drums).

On the night of 21/22 June, The AAF boarded the *Queen Elizabeth*, berthed in dock 90 on the Hudson River in New York, and five days later they arrived in Great Britain, where they were to stay for five and a half months. Although the band was stationed in Bedford, they frequently came to London for performances at the Queensbury All Services Club in New Compton Street, London (now the Prince Edward Theatre), from where some of the BBC broadcasts were transmitted. I was then a member of The Geraldo Orchestra, which was contracted to perform about nine broadcasts a week, and it was during a shared broadcast at the Queensbury Club that Carmen and I first met. We soon became firm friends, and it wasn't long before he showed me the score of 'Two Moods', which he had written in 1942 for guitar solo with orchestral accompaniment. The piece became one of my regular features in The Geraldo Orchestra broadcasts, and I later recorded it on Parlophone, backed by my own composition 'In Charlie's Footsteps', dedicated to Charlie Christian. 'Two Moods' is an excellent representation of Carmen's talents, and since I couldn't find any more of his recorded improvisations when collecting the material for this book, I include it here as an example of his work.

As one can observe from the score, the double-tempo part is improvised, illustrated by only a set of basic chord symbols. This had to be transcribed from the record, as there is no written part in existence, and since it was played over 50 years ago, it must have been well in advance of its time. (Incidentally, in 1991, both 'Two Moods' and 'In Charlie's Footsteps' were reissued on the Music For Pleasure album *At The Swing Shop* [EMI DL1198].)

After the war, Carmen returned to civilian life in his native New York, where he worked successfully as MD, guitarist and arranger, becoming managing director for singer Morton Downey, distinguishing himself on many recordings and, as a member of staff at NBC, New York, taking part in many TV transmissions, including a fashion show broadcast five mornings a week, for which he acted both as musical director and as solo accompanist for many years. Carmen would sit in front of a TV screen at NBC Studios with a pair of headphones over his ears, a guitar in his hands and a music stand in front of him and he would provide the background to the scenes unfolding before him.

Whenever my wife and I went on business visits to New

York, Carmen, his wife, Frankie, and ourselves would go out on the town, and there wasn't a more genial or knowledgeable jazz-music buff. New York will never be the same without him.

Two Moods (Mastren)

Recorded 1945 and released on Parlophone P2105. Reissued on EMI Music For Pleasure 01189 in 1990. Ivor Mairants with Geraldo's Swing Orchestra.

14 CHUCK WAYNE

'Cherokee' (Noble)
'I Surrender, Dear' (Barris and Clifford)

Chuck Wayne (born Charles Jagelka, 1923, died 1997) began playing on the mandolin, and when 'Cherokee' was recorded he had been a professional guitarist for no more than about five years. He became a professional guitarist in 1941, served in the US armed forces from 1942–44 and played with Joe Marsala at the Hickory House, New York, from 1944–46. Thereafter, he was a driving force in The Woody Herman Herd and part of the famous George Shearing Quartet, being the first of Shearing's guitarists to create that original piano/guitar/ vibes block harmony heard in 'East Of The Sun'.

I met Chuck when he came to London for a fortnight in the middle of 1955 to perform the dual role of musical director and accompanist to Tony Bennett, when he borrowed my guitar amplifier. By that time, he was an accomplished jazz player and schooled technician, having taken six months' leave of absence from work in order to perfect his guitar technique.

Chuck embraced the music of Charlie Parker and Dizzy Gillespie very early on and must have been very excited to have been on a recording session with Dizzy, and he shows his complete commitment by his exciting performance, playing at a very fast tempo, almost beyond his technique at the time. Despite his technical failings, Chuck's ear takes him through the minefield of improvisation in the bebop idiom. It may be a little raw in places, but this is evidence of things to come, a milestone in guitar bebop style.

The 64-bar solo opens with a more or less straightforward statement in which the notes follow the chord sequence but in a frantic rhythm that intensifies the phrasing. The surging rhythms (part of the bebop idea) lace the whole solo, thereby heightening the general syncopation. In fact, it's more difficult to transcribe than to appreciate.

The basic harmony of bars nine and ten is B♭, but this becomes B♭6–5 with the inclusion of G and E into the melodic line. Bars eleven and twelve – originally a C7 – become C7–5 with emphasis on the flattened fifth at the beginning of the bar, running into a part whole-tone scale and, in bar twelve, becoming a Gm with a major seventh (ie G, B♭, D and F♯). In bar 13, Chuck takes the easy option by staying in the third position and leading his fingers into a semitone run before running this into finishing this 16-bar section with a more conventional ending.

Bar 17 begins with a breath before Chuck embarks on a new idea, both melodically and rhythmically, no doubt inspired by the close proximity of Dizzy Gillespie, but the next eight bars (25–32) seem to have strained his ingenuity and technical dexterity, as if he were pleased to have reached the halfway point.

The middle 16 bars are almost ingeniously lyrical and illustrate Chuck's melodic inventiveness as, with a change of key, he alters and lifts up the whole mood, while the last 16 bars, although still exciting, revert to a more or less safe coda. The whole solo demonstrates the determination of a young player both to rise to the occasion and to play jazz beyond his era.

Chuck joined Woody Herman in 1946, and at this time he was the guitar soloist on the then-sophisticated 'Summer Sequence', composed and arranged by Ralph Burns. He also introduced some bebop solo guitar, as demonstrated on his solo with The Herman Band on 'I Surrender, Dear', which compares well with Charlie Christian's version.

Chuck left George Shearing in 1952 (when George went commercial) in order to improve his playing, and when he was in London, in 1955, he played on a record issued on the Savoy label (LZ 14014) with The Chuck Wayne Quintet, comprising Zoot Sims, Brew Moore, Harvey Leonard, George Duvivier and Ed Shaughnessy. He then worked at CBS during the '60s, and in 1973 he teamed up with Joe Puma, with whom he recorded some very interesting arrangements. It has always been a mystery to me why he was never nominated in any of the *Down Beat* polls or received any other credits, either by readers or critics, while others of the same age and with no more talent figured much more prominently.

Cherokee (Noble)

Recorded 1 December 1945, New York. Released on Black And White BABW74. Chuck Wayne (guitar) with The Joe Marsala Sextet, including Dizzy Gillespie (trumpet), Cliff Jackson (piano), Irv Lang (bass) and Buddy Christian (drums).

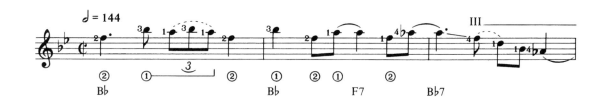

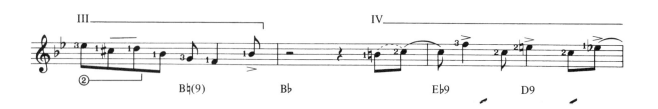

© 1938 Peter Maurice Music Co Ltd, London WC2H oQY. Reproduced by permission of IMP Ltd.

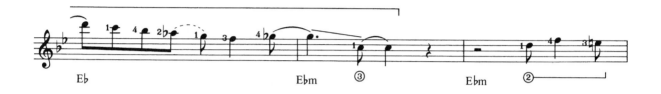

I Surrender, Dear (Barris and Clifford)

Recorded in 1946. Chuck Wayne with Woody Herman.

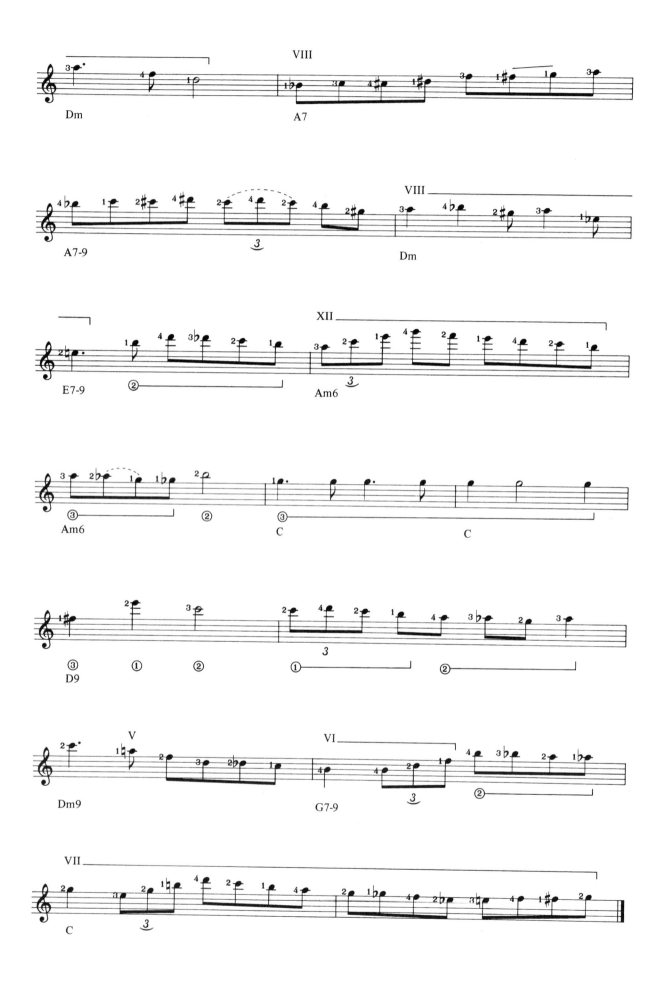

15 BILL DE ARANGO

Another inspirational player worthy of note is Bill De Arango. Born on 20 September 1921, Bill began his musical career in his home town of Cleveland, USA, in around 1939, before being he was drafted into the US forces in 1942. When he was demobbed, in 1944, he became involved in the New York jazz scene, becoming particularly intrigued by the jazz that was then being played by black musicians in the 52nd Street clubs. He was then offered a job by Don Byas, who had heard De Arango playing in a jazz session in one of the clubs.

During his short stay with Byas, the venue in which they were engaged was often visited by Dizzy Gillespie, Charlie Parker and other jazz luminaries who got to know and like his playing, and this no doubt led to him being included on a prestigious Victor recording of *Esquire* poll winners in 1945, during which '52nd Street Theme', 'Night In Tunisia' and other famous titles were recorded. His career continued to be successful until 1948, when he left New York and returned to Cleveland to become involved in the musical-instrument business.

In his recording of '52nd Street Theme' with the Dizzy Gillespie Sextet, recorded in 1945 on HMV B9631 (PO6-V8-1682-1), the material is often scalic, hardly ever shaped in contours or curves or chordal spreads, and is rather minimalistic. Nevertheless, it has an original charm of its own. In fact, if you can find a copy, on closer listening one finds that, although the piece is in the key of C, the first couple of bars contain the first five notes of the scale of A♭ (A♭, B♭, C, D♭ and E♭), and yet the sound is not at all extraneous. This leads me to believe that, in this instance, the notes of the A♭ major scale have been superimposed onto the key of C. For instance, A♭ against a chord of C is the augmented fifth note, B♭ the minor seventh, D♭ a passing note and E♭ a blue note.

In the fourth bar and elsewhere, very good use is made of the dominant chord with the sharpened ninth (G, B, D, F and A♯), but in this bar the chord commences on the sharpened ninth itself (A♯ or B♭) and leads chromatically with a run of B♭, A, G and F down to E♮ (part of the chord of C).

The middle-eight bars begin with a switch from constant quavers to a change of tack with a silent beat. Then, after a passage of D7, the sharpened ninth is again invoked, and instead of commencing with one of the normal notes of the chord (ie D, F♯, A or C), the phrase begins with F♮.

'52nd Street Theme' is really based on any 32-bar tune with a tonic, sub-mediant, supertonic and dominant structure: eight bars repeated, a middle-eight of tonic (C7) resolving to F, ascending to the dominant of the next key up a fifth (D7) and returning to the original key by way of the dominant seventh (G7). In chordal terms:

$$| \text{C} / \text{Dm7} / | \text{Em7} / \text{Dm7} / | \text{⁄} | \text{⁄} |$$
$$\text{Em7} / \text{E♭m7} | \text{Dm7} / \text{D♭9} / \|$$

leading to a middle-eight of:

$$| \text{C9} / / / | \text{⁄} | \text{F} / / / | \text{F} / \text{A7} / | \text{D9} / / / | \text{⁄} |$$
$$\text{G} / / / | \text{(D♭9–5} / / /) \; \text{D♭9–5} / / / |$$

One could impose the melody of 'Blue Moon' as the first, second and last eight-bar phrase, or the more extraneous 'riff' of '52nd Street Theme', with a suitably boplicised middle-eight.

The most notable features of the tune are the notes G♭ or F♯ (ie the flattened fifth or augmented fourth of the scale of C in bar seven) and the last note in bar 24, C♯ or D♭, resolving to C. D♭ is the flattened fifth of G7 (G, B, D♭ and F), ie the flattened fifth of the dominant chord of C. In bar four of the coda, the minor seventh of the tonic, B♭, is employed before finally resolving onto the G♭ or F♯ as the final note. If you can find a recording and listen to the effect that the notes B♭ and G♭ have, it is rather one of disturbance than resolve. In this solo, there is much evidence of the way in which diatonic scales are distorted by means of augmented and diminished intervals.

16 ARV GARRISON

'Tonsillectomy' (Hardy)

Arv Garrison (born 17 August 1922, Toledo, Ohio, died 30 July 1960) began playing the guitar at the age of twelve and fronted his own group in 1941. Later, he played in Pittsburgh in a band led by Don Seat. He also recorded with The Howard McGhee Sextet and with Charlie Parker on *Dial*, on the Spotlight label.

He married bassist Vivien Gary in 1946, with whom he formed The Vivien Gary Trio of guitar, bass and piano. In 1947, they recorded 'Tonsillectomy', played at a very fast tempo, and in complete contrast 'These Foolish Things', the record on which I first heard Arv Garrison play.

His solo on 'Tonsillectomy' was an attempt at bop in the minor, but strictly speaking it was trying to break out of the post-Charlie Christian syndrome and to avoid copying the Gillespie/Parker school. I have no doubt that Garrison was influenced in this respect by George Hardy, the tune's composer, a pianist who loved developing 'modern harmony', ie minor sevenths substituted, augmented and flattened.

George Hardy had a penchant for odd titles like 'Tonsillectomy' and 'Salvatore Sally', which he wrote for Boyd Rayburn's orchestra and which was recorded by them on the Jewel label as one of the titles on an album entitled *Innovations*. In this respect (ie of the development of music), it may be appropriate to quote Ben Pollock, one-time bandleader and now president of Jewel Records: 'Not much longer will [man] be satisfied with band barbershop harmonies or the bag of musical ad lib tricks of the jive five... The order of the day is symphonic jazz music.'

'Tonsillectomy' seems to be an answer to Ben Pollock's plea, and the example improvised by Arv Garrison seems to be in sympathy with the composer but not quite with the player, who has not yet become very familiar with the mixed idiom.

Another piece recorded by Garrison, however, 'These Foolish Things', however, portrays the guitarist at his lyrical and wholly rhapsodic best. On the version recorded in 1947, the very first two bars stamp a firm sense of rhythm, movement and passing substitute harmony at its most entrancing, followed equally well by two bars that substitute the chords of E♭/Cm7 with the much warmer, more engaging chords of F9♯11/E9♯11, which are both more dramatic as well as more chromatic.

The next bar and a half contains a masterly running commentary on the melody, creating a breathing-space before leading into the last two bars of the eight-bar melody using a bar each of F9♯ and E9♯11 to lead chromatically with augmented arpeggios and semitone and whole runs to the second eight bars. The following three bars are again rhapsodic, but the next makes full use of the descending chords F13 and E13 to change from runs to thirds in harmony. The thirds continue and announce the last four bars, and the phrase ends with an appropriate tricky blues phrase, leading into a positive finish on the tonic note of E♭. Altogether, the piece is a kind of rhapsodic, bopish solo reminiscent of George Benson in a slow mood.

Tonsillectomy (Hardy)

Recorded December 1947. Arv Garrison with The Vivien Gary Trio.

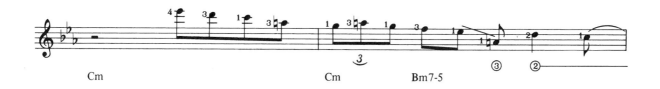

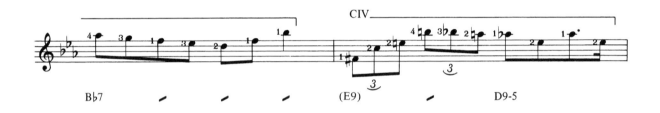

17 BARNEY KESSEL

'Cheers' and 'Carvin' The Bird' (McGhee)

By the time Barney Kessel (born 17 October 1923, Muskogee, Oklahoma) was 30, he had topped the *Down Beat* international critics' poll and, in 1956, the *Down Beat* poll itself. He retained his top rating for five years – no mean feat in that competitive area – and came top in the international critics' poll again in 1959.

In as far back as 1945, he was recording music with Artie Shaw and his Gramercy Five, which included Roy Eldridge, a trumpet player who, in his time, had an advanced jazz style, until the advent of Dizzy Gillespie. Barney should have joined Artie Shaw at the London Festival Hall on 17 June 1992, but sadly he suffered a stroke, a blow to his tremendous *joie de vivre* that later prevented him from performing.

I include this piece as an illustration of Barney's bop aspects. Barney has always had the knack of getting on with any musical group to which he is assigned, whether it's a big band like Artie Shaw's ('Hop, Skip, Jump'); the fantastic Oscar Peterson Quartet; The Great Guitars, with Herb Ellis and Charlie Byrd; or Dizzy Gillespie's and Charlie Parker's groups. Therefore, I consider it important to make the acquaintance of his solos in the various stages of the development of jazz.

In the post-Charlie Christian period of the '40s, when bop was cultivating extended harmonies and inventing lushly syncopated themes of memorable distinction, Charlie Parker and Dizzy Gillespie became leaders of the various recording groups, including in their groups jazz players who were considered to be comfortable bedfellows. (Don't take this too literally!)

Howard McGhee was a contemporary of Charlie Parker, a trumpet player of the Gillespie school and an inventor of themes. 'Cheers' and 'Carvin' The Bird' are two examples. The first is a twelve-bar blues and the second a 32-bar theme of eight bars repeated, an improvised bridge (or middle-eight bars) and a final eight bars. Both themes create excitement by their transient restlessness, coupled with agitated, mercurial elements of phrasing. Although the themes aren't actually written by Charlie Parker, the construction and phrasing are so closely linked with his improvisation that it is obviously inspired by him. If ever a Parker ambience was created, it was in this double theme.

In his two solo passages, Barney Kessel has surely taken up the challenge and moved away from his previous, prolonged Charlie Christian period. Hence he has to be mentioned in different periods just to illustrate how flexible he has been throughout his long and creative career.

Both of these solos place Barney in the bop school of the period while at the same time present him as a melodist. In fact, both themes and guitar solos are, in their way, immensely melodic.

Cheers (McGhee)/Carving The Bird (McGhee and Parker)

Both recorded 26 February 1947 and released on Esquire 10.031 (D1072). Barney Kessel with Charlie Parker's New Stars: Howard McGhee (trumpet), Charlie Parker (alto sax), Wardell Gray (tenor sax), Dodo Marmarosa (piano), Red Callender (bass) and Don Lamond (drums). Supervision: Ross Russell.

Theme 1 with intro

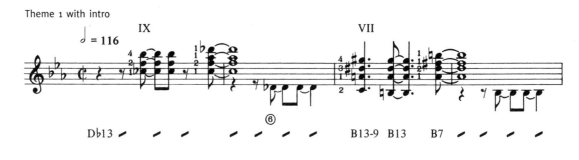

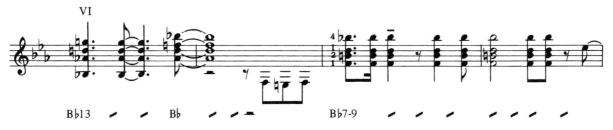

Theme

Barney Kessel's improvisation on Theme 1

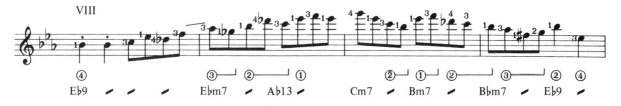

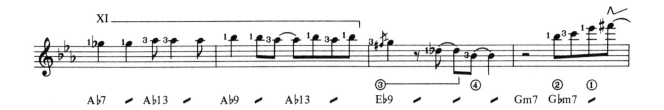

Ab7   Ab13   Ab9   Ab13   Eb9   Gm7   Gbm7

Fm7   Bb13   Bb13/Bb   Eb6/9   Db9   Bb7

Theme 2: 'Carvin' The Bird'

Bb   Cm7   Dm7   Dbm7   Cm7   Gb9

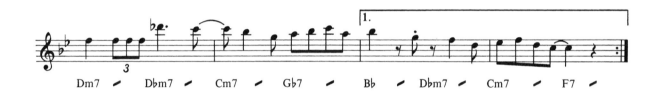

Dm7   Dbm7   Cm7   Gb7   Bb   Dbm7   Cm7   F7

Bb   Cm7   Bb   Fm7   Bb7   Cm6

Bb13   Cm6   C13   C7   C9

Cm7   Cm(maj7)   Cm7   F7   Bb   Cm7   Dm7   Dbm7

Barney Kessel's improvisation on Theme 2

18 OSCAR MOORE

'Sweet Georgia Brown' (The King Cole Trio)

Oscar Moore (born 25 December 1916, Austin, Texas, died 1981) began to play professionally in 1934, at the age of 18. At 21, he joined Nat 'King' Cole's trio and stayed with him for ten years. Recordings with The King Cole Trio made him immensely popular. He was also heard in some lyrical playing in the programme *Midnight From Munich*, where the trio's recordings of 'Gee, Baby, Ain't I Good To You' made a tremendous impression.

In slow numbers, he used various vocal-sounding effects – ie tremoloing in a long, downward glissando – as well as string bending. He would commence a phrase on the higher semitone and release the bend to normal as follows: B♭ on the bent second string (tenth fret) released to A and eventually landing on G (eighth fret) in a real vocal style. He won the *Down Beat* and *Metronome* readers' polls from 1945–48 while he was with Cole, but he left him in 1949 while in Los Angeles and stayed there, being on call at MGM Studios and for other studio work.

Oscar was neither a follower of Charlie Christian nor of the bop school. In fact, his style – although lyrical in slow numbers and technical in fast numbers – was not sufficiently individual in construction to place him as an originator or innovator, if one compares him to Charlie Christian.

There were many good jazz players in the 1940s and, although it's unfair to judge one against the other by the few examples I've selected for publication, there are a number of memorable jazz-guitar improvisations that stand out more than 'Sweet Georgia Brown'. The tempo is very fast, and Moore has taken the option of making a stab at a running commentary, rather than a well-conceived overall plan.

On the other side of 'Sweet Georgia Brown', the trio sings and plays 'It's Better To Be By Yourself' at a medium ♪ = 144. The key is F and the guitar solo commences with a good harmony lead-in in the normal post-Charlie Christian mainstream style, as follows:

So far, so good, but for the next twelve bars nothing very constructive happens, and the trend of the movement is vague. As I said, Oscar was a very good player but no pathfinder or innovator. It was probably his long association with The King Cole Trio that gave him his prominence.

Sweet Georgia Brown (Bernie, Pinkard and Casey)
Recorded 1945 and released on Capitol 239-1653. Oscar Moore with The King Cole Trio.

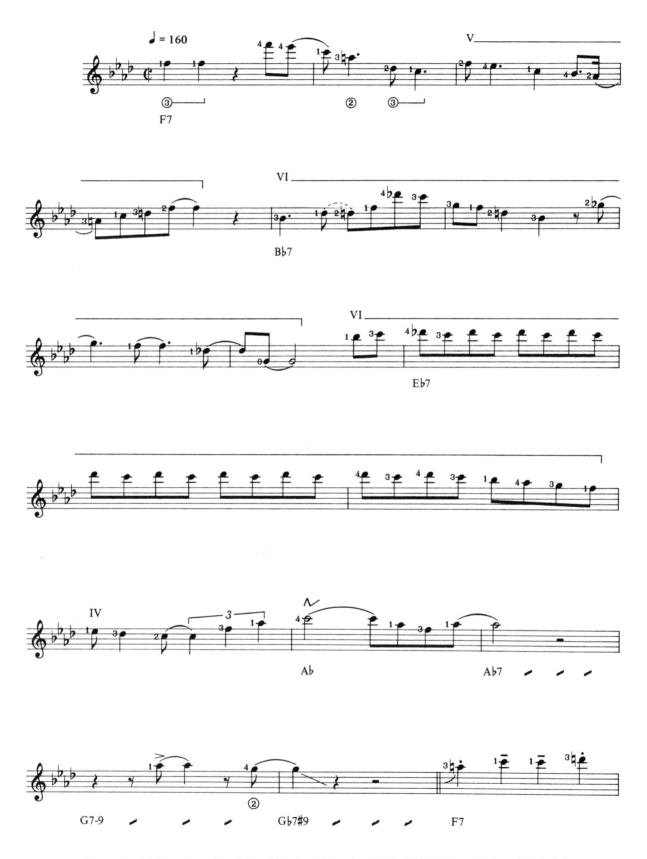

F7
F7#9

III

Bb9

X

Bb9
Fm7
Fm6

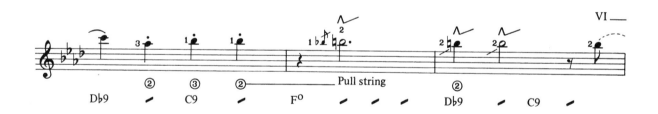

VI

Db9
C9
F°
Pull string
Db9
C9

IV

Ab
Ab7
Ebm6
F7-9
F9

IV

Bbm7
Eb7+5
Ab
C9

19 TONY MOTTOLA

'Guilty' (Kahn and Akst)

Strictly speaking, Tony Mottola (born 18 March 1918) is known not for his jazz but rather for his extremely tasteful solo playing and his recordings with Perry Como, Dinah Shore, Frank Sinatra (with whom he toured as solo accompanist) and The Andrews Sisters. He has also conducted recording sessions for Johnny Desmond on MGM Records and for Burl Ives on Columbia Records and has served as number-one guitarist for CBS.

Mottola's solo chorus in 'Guilty', transcribed from his record, is mainly melodic but is played with such élan, feeling and lyricism that the melodic embellishments are transformed into what may be termed a kind of improvisation. He makes very good tonal use of slurs and choice of strings as well as notes. There are also some substitutions of harmony, although by no means to the extent employed by Arv Garrison.

It's surprising not to find Tony Mottola mentioned in any of the guitar histories that I've read, but he well deserves to be known among guitarists. He was a contemporary of Carmen Mastren, who was also on the staff of studios at CBS and NBC, where they sometimes worked together.

Guilty (Kahn and Akst)

Recorded by Tony Mottola.

20 LES PAUL

'How High The Moon' (Hamilton)

Les Paul (born 9 June 1916, Waukesha, Wisconsin) is far too famous for me to have to gild the lily, except to say that I have been privileged to count him as a good friend since 1952, when he first came to London to top the bill at the London Palladium and performed onstage with his wife at the time, Mary Ford.

One of his big hits was 'How High The Moon', which I have reproduced here as a work for two or three guitars and voice. The recording was, of course, made by Les Paul playing all of the parts himself, first laying down the rhythm and then overdubbing the bass, second guitar, first guitar and, finally, the voice.

When Les presented this revolutionary version to the world, no one else had considered changing the speed of the tape recorder and not only dubbing one part over another but also taking one part up an octave and another down an octave so that the bass notes sounded as if they had been played in the correct bass register.

Anyone who has been able to view the video in which he told the story of the way he developed his musical and electronic technique will have realised the multi-talented genius of Les Paul, guitarist, improviser, entertainer and electronic-recording trickster. If readers can find a copy of this video, I need say no more, but for the many who may like to hear how this loveable genius won his international fame, I will relate some of his story.

He taught himself the guitar and began playing at an early age, if the three-chord trick can be called playing the guitar. When he became a professional, he performed solo under the name Rhubarb Red, because of the colour of his hair. He then teamed up with Joe Wolverton ('Singing Joe'), and in the early '30s he left Waukesha for Chicago, where he stayed for five years, working at local radio stations as both a country-and-western player and a jazz player under his own name of Les Paul.

1939 saw him in New York, where he formed a trio playing electric guitar and secured engagements with Frank Waring and his Pennsylvanians. He had earlier experimented with the electric guitar and discovered that, in order to produce a sustained sound of a controlled nature, the body of the guitar, rather than being hollow, should be solid. He proceeded to prove this by fixing a thick plank of wood to the fingerboard and fitting a pick-up to the guitar. In fact, this invention – attached to which were two imitation guitar-shaped sides – became known as 'the plank'.

Les later spent time in Hollywood, where he recorded with Bing Crosby, Gene Autrey, Jack Benny and The Andrews Sisters, and it was Crosby who encouraged him to build a recording studio. Between his experiments with the electric guitar and his winning the *Down Beat* readers' poll in 1951, 1952 and 1953, his name shot to fame, first with his trio and then with his multitrack recordings, from which I've selected 'How High The Moon'.

In 1946, Les built his own studio and began to experiment with multitracking. In 1949, he met and married the singer Colleen Summers (Mary Ford). When he appeared at the London Palladium with her in 1952, he played one of the first Gibson Les Paul solid guitars with a tremolo arm.

It had been a long, uphill struggle for him to persuade Messrs Gibson to enter into this field. (Their reputation as the makers of the world's finest-sounding arch-top f-hole acoustic guitars was unsurpassed.) In the end, though, they reached a compromise with Les. They would produce this electric guitar but, rather than christen it with the name of Gibson, they would instead call it the Les Paul guitar made by Gibson. This proposition was accepted by Les and of course gave him a lifelong stake in the instrument and lifelong royalties.

The solid-body guitar nevertheless took another decade to become popular, but with the advent of rock, Eric Clapton and the solid-body craze the Gibson Les Paul guitar became (together with the Fender Stratocaster) one of the most copied guitars in the world.

Musically, Les Paul – who doesn't read music – has always been attracted to the playing of Django Reinhardt, and when I became intrigued by Paul's playing, in as early as 1946, I wrote about his recordings in an article for *Melody Maker*, stating that the style of his solo in 'Blue Skies' (Brunswick 3656A) was reminiscent of Reinhardt. However, it wasn't until we met again, in 1973, that I discovered that Les had been one of Django's greatest admirers. Les had, in fact, made a pilgrimage to Paris to meet the man, only to be told that he wasn't there at the time. In desperation, Les had asked a co-operative taxi driver to try to locate Django, handing him part of a $5 bill that he had torn in half, with the promise of the other half when he returned with the required information. In due course, the taxi driver returned, collected the other half of the bill and drove Les to Fontainebleau, where Django greeted him with open arms. Django died in 1953, and when Les discovered that no suitable stone had been erected over his grave, he had a special tombstone made and erected.

It's remarkable that Les Paul was able to continue building up his outstanding career, for, as he told me in 1952, it was abruptly halted a few years earlier by a severe car accident in which he broke almost every bone in his body. However, after many operations, his right arm and elbow were reassembled. His mobility was very limited, though, and he had to pick the guitar from a lower angle, forcing him to hang the instrument lower than before.

He seems to have retired from public performances in the late '60s, although when I met him in Chicago during the 1973 Music Trade Fair he sounded as cheerful as ever, and when I visited the 1975 NAMM show his playing on the Gibson stand hadn't lost any of its lustre. We met again later that year, when I was invited to hear him give a concert at the Excelsior Hotel at London's Heathrow Airport, and this time he was using his Les Paulvariser guitar in conjunction with a pre-recorded tape. It was sensational!

In January 1989, *Guitar Player* magazine featured 'A Celebration Of Les Paul', who for the previous five years had been playing on a weekly basis at Fat Tuesday's in New York to packed audiences, which included at one time or another George Benson, Tal Farlow, Herb Ellis, Jimmy Page, Mark Knopfler, Johnny Smith, Eddie Van Halen, Al Di Meola and Steve Miller. His records have sold over 100 million copies and he is still one of the greatest performers, showmen, entertainers and inventors of our time.

How High The Moon (Hamilton)

Released on Capitol CL13505. Les Paul (guitar) and Mary Ford (vocals).

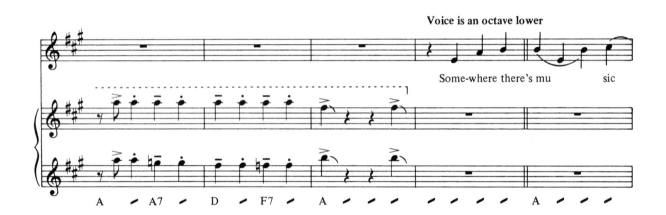

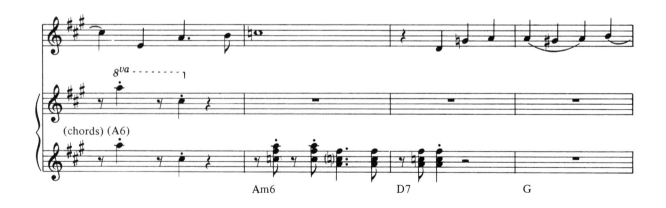

21 BILLY BAUER

'September In The Rain' (Dubin, Warren and Dunn)
'What Is This Thing Called Love' (Porter)

William Henry Bauer (born 14 November 1915, New York City) is one of a number of musicians born at around the same time who began on the banjo and later transferred to the guitar.

He was a well-known dance-band guitarist and played in Abe Lyman's orchestra, a very prominent American band during the '30s, after Lyman had appeared at the London Kit-Kat Restaurant and the London Palladium. In fact, there is an extremely tenuous link between Abe Lyman's guitarist and myself, albeit a tenuous one, as Roy Fox, who was born in Denver in 1901 and for whom I worked from 1933–37, joined Abe Lyman at the age of 18.

Billy Bauer joined The Woody Herman Band in 1944 and stayed until 1946, which gave him a very good standing among guitarists. He then freelanced with Benny Goodman and Chubby Jackson and became very interested in free-form jazz after meeting Lennie Tristano, from whom he learned a great deal. Lennie was the foremost player and advocate of free-form jazz, and many of his records feature Billy Bauer, who wove textures into Tristano's free-form piano in 'Through These Portals'/'Speculation' with The Lennie Tristano Quartet (Melodisc N32) and 'I Can't Get Started' and 'Yesterdays' with The Lee Konitz Sextet (Capitol CL13456).

Lee Konitz (alto) was also prominent in this free-form style and Billy recorded a number of duets with him, including 'Rebecca' (Esquire 10-175) and 'Ice Cream Konitz', with The Lee Konitz Quintet. He was also fond of playing old standards to bop settings, and I have therefore included 'What Is This Thing Called Love', with Lee Konitz, as well as 'September In The Rain', on which one of his favourites, 'Marionette', is based.

'Marionette' itself is in the key of E♭. In the first two bars, the melodic line assumes a changed complexion from the original melody to 'September In The Rain', by beginning on D (the major seventh of E♭) and leading up to E♭ before leading to F and E (the ninth and minor ninth, respectively,

of the chord E♭7–9), rising by a diminished run (G, B♭, D♭, E) and finally dropping by a semitone to reach the E♭ in the third bar. If you can find a transcription, the G in the fourth bar is the major seventh of the chord of A♭. Although the chord in bar five is A♭m6, the D♭ at the very apex of the A♭m run (A♮, E♭, F) transforms the sound to B♭7–9/11♯9, which is more restless and exciting. In bar six, the G against the A♭m6 gives the note a much more unresolved character than the G in bar four (A♭maj7). It is similar to D♭9–5, so that the G exudes a bop character. Although the melody note in bar eight is B♭ (ie the dominant note of the key), the G♮ in the harmony (E7♯9) produces another type of dissonance.

The harmonic construction of a tune like 'Subconscious Lee', however, is quite different. This piece is in the key of C and begins with C7 going to Fm6, then G7 to C major. Despite the change of sequence, a flattened fifth in the context of C7 is still boppish. In bar one, the emphasised F♯ in the chord of C7 still provides an unsettled sound and in bar two there is both the flattened fifth (F♯) and the augmented fifth (G♯), followed by the tonic (C) and the minor seventh (B♭), thus producing a piquant dominant-to-tonic (minor) resolution. The B♮ leading into bar five is a foretaste of G7, upon which it resolves.

The ascending/descending run in bar six is commonplace but attractive and is often used when the dominant harmony – either G7+ or D♭13 – leads to C major, as it does here. But it is not as commonplace when used as a flattened fifth (F♯), as it is in bar seven of this piece, against a chord of C, especially on an accented beat. (Bauer must have been fond of this F♯, for he uses it again in the context of a C9 chord in bar nine.)

Bauer's esoteric playing career eventually got through to the wider jazz enthusiasts when, in 1949 and 1950, he was voted top of the poll by *Down Beat*'s readers. Although his phrases haven't been copied, in the manner of Django Reinhardt, Charlie Christian or Wes Montgomery, his style is original and well worth studying.

September In The Rain (Dubin, Warren and Dunn)
Arranged for guitar by Ivor Mairants. Published by B Feldman & Co.

What Is This Thing Called Love (Porter)

Arranged for guitar by Ivor Mairants.

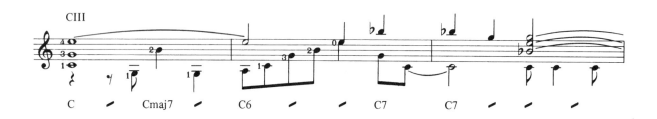

22 PETE CHILVER

In his youth, Pete Chilver (born 1924, Slough) was attracted to the guitar and, particularly, to jazz. By the time he was 16, he had established his own small group of semi-pros, although by trade he was a draughtsman and was working in an engineering factory. Jazz pianist Ralph Sharron was pursuing a similar occupation in a nearby factory and was also the leader of a small band somewhat in competition with his neighbours, so it came as no surprise when Pete and Ralph joined forces and formed one band. Shortly afterwards, they entered a *Melody Maker* dance-band contest and were awarded first prize for their respective instrumental abilities. One adjudicator happened to be a Belgian jazz trumpet player called Johnny Claes, who, having discovered two such outstanding jazz players, soon had them playing in his own band on various gigs, including the Feldman Club, London's leading jazz club at the time.

Ralph Sharon was then called up to the RAF, while Pete continued to work in the factory and play around the home counties until the end of the war. By 1946, many of the service personnel had returned to Civvy Street, among them drummer and vocalist Ray Ellington, who established a jazz quartet in which he included Pete Chilver and vibraphonist Tommy Pollard. They began an engagement at the famous (or should that read notorious?) Bag O' Nails night club in Kingley Street, off Regent Street. This was the start of a professional career that lasted until 1950. During those four short years, Chilver created a stir in the London jazz business, being voted Top Guitarist in the *Melody Maker* poll of 1949, with Dave Goldberg second and me third, although in the 1947 poll Dave Goldberg came first, I was second and Pete came third. However, out of sight, out of mind, as illustrated by the 1950–1 poll, which again placed me first and Pete third. So much for the fickle fans!

During his short but meteoric professional flight, Pete joined Tito Burns in 1947, and he was also a member of The Jack Parnell Quartet and Organisation, a member of Ted Heath's band and finally joined Ambrose before forsaking the musical profession for a successful career in the catering business. Nevertheless, Pete Chilver's contemporaries have always considered him to be the leading bop guitarist of his time.

If they are still available, I would direct the reader to transcripts of two of Chilver's recordings: 'More Than You Know' and 'Take The A-Train' (the latter published by Campbell Connolly in *Bebop Arrangements Of Six World-Famous Tunes*). In these two contrasting pieces, Chilver demonstrates his commitment to boppery and a refusal to be hidebound by it. In the former, the overall result emphasises a bop variation of the chords of the piece instead of a melodic invention, and the flowing phrases suggest a connection with melody. If you can find a transcript, you'll see that the Dm7-D♭7-C progression of the then-current Parker/Gillespie school is also invoked at a time when this was still considered to be new music.

In contrast, in the latter piece, 'Take The A-Train', few bebop clichés are used, and in places the piece is vaguely reminiscent of the Charlie Christian school. It was published in 1941 and an important phrase in the melody (that is, bars two and three of the eight-bar theme) contains an important basic bop ingredient, which is the jump from high E down to G♯ over a chord of D9–5. This ingredient includes the augmented fifth (C to G♯) and the flattened fifth (C, E, F♯ [G♭]). It's not surprising, therefore, that players seized upon this whole-tone construction in order to produce a rhythmic arpeggio, as used in the solo in this piece (bars three to four, eleven, 27–8). Another cliché consists of two heavily emphasised quarter-notes in bars seven and 19, as well as the use of the aforementioned progression of G7-D♭7-C. In those far-off days of the '40s and '50s, adopting such a firm commitment to bebop was to the exclusion of blue notes, or bends, in an attempt to break away from the immediate past of the swinging '30s. Currently, players use every jazz device of the past, present and future, and interpretation is warmer than it was in the bop era.

23 LOUIS STEWART

'Here's That Rainy Day' (Van Heusen)

Although Louise Stewart (born 5 January 1944, Waterford, Ireland) lives in Dublin, he occasionally tours England, and in September and October 1989 he could be heard in London in concert with Frank Evans. For a modest man, his fame has reached far and wide, from recording with Bobby Shew and his group in Hollywood to one of his latest DC recordings in Norway.

When I asked him how I should represent him musically in this book of great guitarists, he retorted drily, 'Why don't you ask one of the great guitarists?'

'So what's the most thrilling thing that's happened to you?' I asked.

'Catching a twelve-pound salmon,' came back the immediate retort.

Seriously, however, his most thrilling musical experiences include playing with the great Tubby Hayes and the 'inspirational' lead radiated by George Shearing that he felt when recently working in his group. Having worked with George myself over 40 years ago, I can absolutely endorse this.

Louis once left a large book of modes in my store and, being a peripatetic travelling musician, said that was unable to collect it for months. I ended up keeping hold of it for over 20 years ago. Since it was fashionable to turn to modal styling in the '80s (ie 'The Visit' by Pat Martino), I asked Louis if he found the modes useful with his improvisations. Having studied them at the time to some effect, he came to the conclusion that one could make too much of a fetish of superimposing modes, so he eventually settled on good melodic lines before allowing the modes to take over.

However, his main consideration is to swing, and to hear him in full flight is to realise that Louis certainly swings.

Louis was introduced to the music of Delius by George Shearing, and he says that it was like discovering a new form of music. His horizons then broadened to include Debussy, Ravel and Bartók. He even confesses to being able to occasionally substitute fingers for pick.

In order to convey the versatility of Louis Stewart, I have chosen one of his most contrasting solos, 'Here's That Rainy Day', a solo in rhapsodic style. This is an interesting arrangement, played in a rubato style, from which the student can learn many clichés inspired by the progressions and clichés originated and used by a host of leading players of the past 40 or 50 years. Most predominantly, however, one is reminded of Joe Pass, who also recorded 'Here's That Rainy Day' in a version in which the first chorus is played out of tempo.

The fill-ins at the ends of phrases here are reminiscent of other rhapsodic arrangements, and the moving bass notes, followed by a chord melody moving around the cycle of fourths, or in chromatic form, are very reminiscent of other players of the era. Some of the long-running cadenzas, however, don't run very smoothly, and some are phrased haphazardly.

All manner of scales are used – minor seventh, major seventh, diminished and augmented – and this adds up to very interesting listening, but the piece lacks a smooth flow and is guilty of some halting phrasing, due to what seems to be uncertainty of immediacy in the improvisatory passages. Nevertheless, it is full of ideas and is worth studying.

Here's That Rainy Day (Van Heusen)

Recorded in 1975 and released on *Louis The First* (SHALP 147). The Louis Stewart Trio.

149

SOME NOTES ON TECHNIQUE

The subject of 'how to…' always seems to feature in guitar books, even the most technically advanced, and there is a good reason for this. Unlike the piano keyboard, on which each note has its designated position, most notes on stringed instruments can be played in more than one position on the fingerboard. On the guitar, this applies to all of the notes on the fingerboard above A (below the stave) and the notes between low A and high E on the twelfth fret of the first string. This means that, on many occasions, the choice of fingering is of great importance, so first of all here is a simple explanation of left-hand fingering.

Fingering

Throughout this book, the index finger is indicated by the figure 1, the middle finger by 2, the ring finger by 3 and the little finger by the figure 4.

In addition to the fingering, there are two other indications by which the guitar score may be marked. These are positions at which notes or chords are to be played, indicated by Roman numerals (I, II, III, IV, V and so on) above the notes or chords and by a ringed number under the notes.

Example 1, below, shows passage complete with fully annotated fingering.

Example 1

Fingering (ie 1, 2, 3, 4) may appear before, above or below the notes

Phrasing

Correct phrasing requires the accurate co-ordination of the left and right hands in the articulation of musical passages and is essential if you want to be able to play with expression. It's also necessary to understand the terms and signs used to express the music you're attempting to perform. In this respect, I would advise readers to buy a book of musical rudiments, preferably *The Rudiments And Theory Of Music*, published by the Associated Board of the Royal Schools of Music.

However, there are some techniques associated with the guitar (although not always uniquely so) that aren't yet represented by universally agreed signs. Many of these are for string bending, although the signs for hammer-ons and pull-offs have now become standardised.

In the following list, you will find the relevant signs for the effects commonly used by guitarists, followed by a couple of musical examples showing some of the signs in use. Some of these signs are in general use, while others are my own creation.

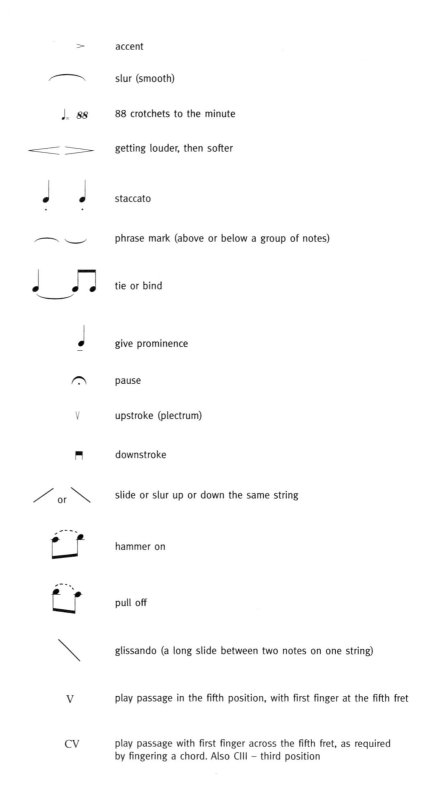

>	accent
⌒	slur (smooth)
♩= 88	88 crotchets to the minute
< >	getting louder, then softer
♩ ♩	staccato
⌒ ⌣	phrase mark (above or below a group of notes)
♩ ♫	tie or bind
♩	give prominence
⌢	pause
V	upstroke (plectrum)
⊓	downstroke
╱ or ╲	slide or slur up or down the same string
	hammer on
	pull off
╲	glissando (a long slide between two notes on one string)
V	play passage in the fifth position, with first finger at the fifth fret
CV	play passage with first finger across the fifth fret, as required by fingering a chord. Also CIII – third position

Example 2

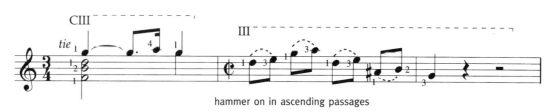

hammer on in ascending passages

Example 3

pull off in descending passages

slur or slide (portamento)

String Bending

By bending – ie pulling or pushing the string sideways across the fingerboard – and picking the note before the string is bent, the picked note can be raised a semitone or more, producing a 'blue note'. (See diagram [A].)

By bending the string before striking the note, striking the string and then releasing the tension, the note will descend by a semitone. The left-hand finger must retain the normal pressure behind the fret. (See diagram [B].)

The following passage (Example 4, below) involves upward and downward semitones, but prescribes bending instead of sliding. To play it, place the third finger on the eleventh fret of the third string (F♯). Play F♯, then bend the string sideways until it reaches G, but don't release it until you've prepared the B♭ on the second

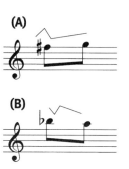

string. Place the second finger on the tenth fret of the second string and bend up to B♭, but don't strike until the string is bent. Play the B♭ (the 'blue note') and revert to the original position at the tenth fret, the B♭ descending to A, which should sound without further picking from the right hand.

Example 4

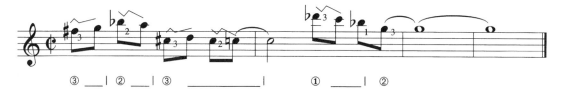

To recap, the symbol in diagram (C) tells you to bend the string to reach the semitone above, while that in diagram (D) means that, having bent the string to the semitone above the fingered note, you should release to revert to the semitone below, ie the actual note.

Grace Notes

In music theory, some notes are known as grace notes, or ornaments. These are used to embellish the principal notes and a list of them can be found in *The Rudiments And Theory Of Music*. However, ornaments are very much dependent on the context in which they occur. In jazz, they are treated accordingly, so that the music in Example 5 is played as shown in Example 6 over the page.

Instead of the broken dotted line shown in Example 7, a more 'blues' effect can be produced by bending the string. Play the basic note, bend the string up one semitone and then release the string to its original note. Another version of the same bend is shown in Example 8. This bend can also be played in reverse, as shown in Example 9. Start this one by preparing the higher note (A♭), release one semitone to G and, without releasing the pressure, bend the string again up to A♭ and release again down to G.

The Great Jazz Guitarists 1

Example 5

Example 6

Example 7

Example 8

Example 9

The art of creating 'blue' notes by bending strings has advanced a great deal since the time of Eddie Lang and Lonnie Johnson. Thinner strings and lower string action now permit bending of more than one semitone.

Bending is now here to stay, but sadly the signs for bending are not. The signs used in this book are of my own creation and are, in my opinion, brief and positive. Hopefully, guitarists will also find them so. Here is a brief recap.

Play first note and bend to fret above.

Prepare first note (B♭), play and then release to fret below, which should sound without further picking.

(G)

Play first note, bend to fret above and release to original fret below, with an accent on the third (principal) note. The first two notes act as grace notes.

(H)

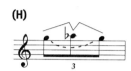

As diagram (G), but with accent on first note.

(I)

A double bend. Prepare as diagram (F), play and bend up and down again without further picking.